A Special
Kind of Love

Robert W. Buckingham

A SPECIAL KIND OF LOVE

Care of the Dying Child

CONTINUUM • NEW YORK

1983

The Continuum Publishing Company
575 Lexington Avenue
New York, New York 10022

Printed in the United States of America

Library of Congress Cataloging in Publication Data

Buckingham, Robert W.
  A special kind of love.

  Bibliography: p. 165
  1.Terminally ill children—Psychology. 2. Death—
Psychological aspects. 3. Terminally ill children—
Family relationships. I. Title.
RJ47.5.B83 1983   155.9'37   82-22073
ISBN 0-8264-0229-1

Dedicated to
the spirit and memory
of
my mother

Contents

Foreword

I am happy to contribute in a small way to Dr. R.W. Buckingham's new book, *A Special Kind of Love: Care of the Dying Child.* Much has been written in recent years about this relatively new field of child thanatology, but there is still relatively little for the parents and health care givers of these little children who need so much of our understanding and comprehension in following their physical changes, as well as their emotional growth and turmoil.

I have known Bob for many years and remember him as a courageous man at the time when he was the first director of research at the first hospice in the United States, the one in New Haven. Although his own research projects stirred up a lot of emotions and a stormy response, he stuck it out and showed the professional community how much work still needed to be done in this area of the care of dying patients.

This helpful book considers many special aspects of this field, from the different concepts children have about death to the special needs and problems of the dying teenager.

Parents and teachers are the most important adults in the lives of these little ones. It is important that grown-ups share this special time with these children and understand that although terminally ill children may be retarded in their physical growth and development, they may far exceed the parents and health care professionals in inner knowledge and wisdom.

"Should we tell the child?" should never be an issue. Rather, we should ask: "Can I hear my child and answer honestly?" If adults would understand the symbolic language of their children and not allow their own pain and guilt to interfere in the communications, the latter could become a unique gift, long remembered after the death of a child. They can also become the teachers of the child's peers and siblings, as long as siblings are not neglected and are not made to feel guilty for their frequent resentment of the sick child, who may no longer be disciplined and who may get all the special treats and gifts the brothers and sisters always wanted.

Yes, to share the life of a dying child can become a gift, but we often see this only much later, when the shock and pain, the loss and the guilt have ebbed, and the memory and the love have endured.

Elisabeth Kübler-Ross

Preface

Death will always be among us. We shall never escape it. Dying is part of the process of living. We must not fear it. We must not hide it. We must not ignore it. We must not deny it. Death is.

The death of a child is considered by many as one of the greatest tragedies on earth. The life of a young flower is taken away. It is a time for sadness, for we believe that the child and the family have been cheated by this sudden disappearance from humanity. Are we not all temporary leaves of the tree of life that someday must fall? Do not leaves fall in springtime as they do in autumn? The child who is understood and loved can give understanding and love no matter how long that child has to live.

We must not protect our children from the reality of death. Death is that process of living that must be faced by both adults and children. We must not deny death.

I write this book then not for scholars, but first and foremost for the parents and relatives who have faced the loss of a child or will be facing an impending loss. I write also for teachers, counselors, and allied health professionals. This book is intended to provide useful information for a specific readership with a common concern: the care of the dying child.

Dr. Elliot Luby states that "when your parent dies you have lost your past. When your child dies you have lost your future." The greatest test of courage we face is not the death of a child, but the courage to live each day as fully as possible. We must not get lost in our grief. We must search out the pathways to courage so that we can continue to live and enjoy the wonders of the world around us.

I have no magic solutions to the mystery of death. There are no simple answers. We health professionals must direct our knowledge and compassion to the difficulties faced by many of our patients and families. We must never separate patients from families nor death from life. They are the horse and carriage of humanity. Rejoice with each new day.

By seeing the world through the eyes of the dying, we can achieve a new kind of understanding of life. The hundreds of dying patients I have worked with have given me a special understanding of and outlook on the true meaning of life. No longer are these people concerned with the trivia that weigh on our shoulders, e.g., bills, errands, petty annoyances. They are concerned with living each day as fully as possible. Now I too try to face each day as a new adventure with the eagerness to make it fully worthwhile for myself, as well as those with whom I come into contact.

I thank Leah Loveday, a gentle and compassionate woman, for her touching piece on the loss of her son David. It has been a joy to work with Leah. Her account adds great depth and meaning to my book.

I thank Elisabeth Kübler-Ross for her inspiration and leadership in this field and her dedication to children and families facing difficult times.

It has been ten years since I first became involved in the hospice movement in this country. In 1973 I became director of research for the first hospice in the United States. My days were spent interviewing and talking with patients (and their families) who had a prognosis of less than three months. I grew to love them. They taught me about the importance of living. I grew in many ways, but most important, in my appreciation of life.

We must remember that the greatest tragedy in life is not that we are going to die; the tragedy is that it is not lived.

I have spent the last two years with dying children. They have a special contribution to make to the existing literature and practice of nursing and medicine.

I will always cherish the memory of a beautiful, blond, five-year-old boy named Jarwin, who had less than a month to live. I asked him if he felt angry or sad that he was dying. I asked him if he felt cheated. He quietly looked at me with his big beautiful eyes, and with the wisdom of an elder he stated, "You know, Dr. Buckingham, nothing is forever." I was awed. He moved me with his simple wisdom. Other children came after Jarwin, and they too are the reason I write this book.

As I write it is early August, an exceptionally cool morning at my Connecticut summer home. The morning mist is circling the lovely old oaks and hemlocks. I wonder the fate of the book. Will it touch people? Can it contribute to a better understanding and practice of care for the dying child? I hope so.

Killingworth, Connecticut
August 1982

1

Fear of Death

"Now this bell tolling softly for another,
says to me, Thou must die."
—John Donne

The solace of sleep offers no protection against it; the companionship of caring friends cannot conquer it; the strength of the human
will is powerless against it. Omnipresent, it can strike with or without warning. It surrounds us and yet we cannot touch it. Faced
with the unalterable fate of our life, we come to fear our invincible
mortal enemy—death.

This dread of death appears universal; almost every person fears
death, albeit to varying degrees. What, then, is the nature of such
a fear? Is the fear of death instinctive, cultural, or a combination of
the two? Evidence suggests the answer is a complex one in which
many factors contribute to an individual's death fear. The universality of the fear cannot be overlooked, yet we must also consider
the vast and varying experiences to which every person is exposed;
there is no simple answer to the question of origin. Personal fear of
death, in general, may stem from an innate framework of human
nature and yet remain modifiable by cultural and social systems.

Analysis of fear is confounded by the "chicken-egg dilemma."
Many people have very specific fears about death and dying. Do
these fears constitute the general fear of death, or does the general
death fear itself create these specific fears? For example, the fear of
the unknown has often been used to explain the origin of the
death fear. Almost as often, the fear of death has been used to ex-

plain the origin of the fear of the unknown. Whatever the answer, we should be aware of this irresolvable dilemma when evaluating the roots of fear.

Examining the way in which different people view death may help us to understand the mechanism through which fear is developed or repressed. Do those with different occupations fear death differently? Is there a substantial difference between those strongly affiliated with religion and those who are not? Perhaps differences and similarities between various cultures will allow us to make inferences regarding the origin of the fear of death.

Influence of Cultural and Social Values

Birth and death are significant moments in the ongoing life of social groups. Birth and death serve as symbols of transition and change, and social rituals and special practices are used by groups to identify the rites of passage associated with the gain or loss of a member. All human societies have developed one or more cultural systems to help their members come to terms with and adapt to the personal and social meanings of death.

Orientations toward death in any society are expressions of the general character of the culture of that society. In the United States, death expectations and attitudes have been greatly influenced by the dominant values of the white, Anglo-Saxon, middle-class culture, which stresses mastery over nature, emphasis on future-time orientation, and an activity orientation of doing instead of simply being or becoming. The individual's personal meaning of death is also influenced by cultural and social conditions: the amount of direct exposure a person has to death and dying, his membership in an ethnic subgroup, and his membership in a particular religious denomination.

Death expectations and attitudes of people in the United States have been affected by four important conditions. First, people tend to equate death with being old. The increase in longevity has caused people to transpose death from an immediate and ever-present menace to a distant and remote prospect. In a country that places a high value on youth and childhood, to die as a child is to die out of phase. Such deaths are conceived as having a high social loss. Second, persons who are ill and elderly tend to be removed to special institutions and communities, so, in general, Americans are insulated from perceptions of death and direct experiences with persons who are dying. Third, the vast growth in scientific knowledge and applied technology in this century has created the expectation that death, too, can be defeated if enough time, money, and energy are applied to solving the problem. Finally, people no longer participate in a society that is dominated by tradition, by lineage and kinship ties, or by accepted dogma. These factors have been replaced by a concept of individual freedom, which has been accompanied by a sense of personal responsibility and increased levels of anxiety.

These changes have led to a depersonalization and fragmentation of the experience of human death. Such a system serves to protect society from the disruptive influences of death by separating the dying from the living and developing bureaucratic procedures for managing death and dying as routine social matters. Psychologically, parents who are facing the loss of a child, and other members of the family, are not prepared for effective performance in the changing roles and role relationships that the event of death brings.

Death Anxiety

In order to focus on the origins of the fear of death, we must first examine in detail the meaning of death fear. Death itself is a very complex and elusive concept; it means many things to many people. It is no surprise, then, that the "fear of death" is actually a complex group of related fears. This complexity of intertwined units constitutes "death anxiety." When we speak of the fear of death in the general sense, we are referring to this elaborate and convoluted meaning. Death anxiety can be subdivided into the fear of death as an event and the fear of dying, each of which has a multitude of subcategories.

Death as an Event

We may feel anxious about accepting a new job because we do not know how it will affect our future. We may profit and succeed or lose and fail, but the lack of certainty creates anxiety. Similarly, we do not know what awaits us after death; it is a complete mystery that most probably will never be solved. Fear of the unknown is very strong, and fear of death, the "unknown of unknowns," is even more so. The cliché "ignorance is bliss" does not apply; in this case ignorance breeds anxiety.

The fear of the dead is merely an extension of the fear of the unknown. Ignorant of the fate of the deceased's spiritual being, we come to fear the corpse. Modern aversion to the dead body is exemplified in stories of ghosts, haunted houses, and cemeteries. By making light of the subject, we are able to express our fear in a socially acceptable manner and thus alleviate some of our repressed death anxiety.

As with most departures, farewells are often the most difficult. Leaving home, friends, and life's small pleasures behind may be a very trying experience. The dread of separation or isolation—and death is the ultimate isolation—leads many to fear death. Just as we may miss old friends when we move to a new home, we will miss friends, relatives, and the security they afford when we die. We will miss the beauty of nature. Fear of separation from such pleasures occupies the minds of many when contemplating the consequences of death. In today's fast-paced society, we often fail to appreciate the little joys life offers. The dying person, forced to think in earnest about the separation death can bring, will often relinquish those things that are extraneous to enjoy the subtle pleasures. Maybe the dying can teach us to be more aware of life as it truly is, to take nothing for granted and to enjoy each day as much as possible. This may seem contradictory: won't we fear separation (and death) more when we have more to lose? On the contrary, those who have lived their life to the fullest fear death less than those who feel they have missed something. The fear of separation in death, then, has two main features: separation means loss of friends, family, and life's pleasures, but it also represents a point beyond which no other chance will be given to enjoy life. Both features of separation lead to a fear of death.

To an extent we are in control of our actions; we are capable of thought and our decision can substantially alter our fate. Death means a loss of consciousness, a loss of self-mastery. Accompanying death is a loss of supremacy and uniqueness; death is the great equalizer. Just as an elected official might fear a political opponent who poses a threat to his power and position, we may fear death, the ultimate threat to our elevated status amongst nature's animals.

> Man is literally split in two: he has an awareness of his own splendid uniqueness in that he sticks out of nature with a towering majesty, and yet goes back into the ground a few feet in order blindly and dumbly to rot and disappear forever. It is a terrifying dilemma to be in and to have to live with . . . to live a whole lifetime with the fate of death haunting one's dreams and even the most sun-filled days.[1]

Social upbringing teaches that wrongs will not go unpunished. A "naughty" child will often wait with intense anxiety for the expected punishment. Since adults sometimes are unable to feel absolved from wrongdoing, they may feel guilty and wait anxiously for a punishment from God. Some view death as such a punishment. Others fear hell and eternal damnation as their castigation. As with the child, anticipation of the punishment (creating fear and anxiety) may affect a person more than the actual chastisement.

With the loss of a loved one, family and friends become emotionally distraught; but the death also affects them in a more concrete way. The death of the head of the household will result in lowered family income and will affect the life style of the surviving dependents. People who support others (either financially or emotionally) frequently fear what will happen to their dependents.

An important point to ponder is the inevitability of death. If death were not inevitable, but "something that happened to an unlucky few," then our entire death fear would be drastically affected. Every time a plane takes off there is a chance it will crash; yet few of us worry when we fly in a plane. In much the same way, if death were only a possibility, we would fear it much less. The fact that death will definitely touch each and every one of us contributes greatly to our overall fear.

Specific fears people have about death as an event have been noted. They include the fear of the unknown, the fear of separation, fear of losing self-mastery and uniqueness, fear of punishment, fear of leaving dependents helpless, and fear of the inevitable. The process of death arouses different fears, fears associated with dying.

Death as a Process
"It is not death I fear but dying."
—Montaigne

Our society has a rather annoying tendency to label its members: people are white or black, male or female, wealthy or poor. The "dying" are thought to be a minority who aren't quite normal by our standards. This categorical separation is due in part to society's communal fear of death; many of us have experienced an uneasy feeling when in the company of a dying person. We cannot face our own death let alone the dying agony of another person. In order to escape the uncomfortable, uneasy feeling we have for the dying, we too frequently isolate and separate them from our lives. When everyone begins to shun them, the dying feel abandoned. Subconsciously, we realize our tendency to isolate the dying and, therefore, fear dying ourselves lest we be abandoned. Dying is a very lonesome activity, a very personal affair. The fear of abandonment is magnified in this time of crisis when the comfort and support of loved ones is so desperately needed.

The majority of people associate pain with the dying process, often because they know of somebody who died after a long, agonizing illness. Many feel that death is the ultimate injury or illness and assume that, since minor illness or injury can be painful, death must be even more painful. This need not always be true, however, since modern medicine is better able to control an individual's pain.

Yet we instinctively avoid suffering and any condition that increases even the probability of pain.

When the process of dying extends over a long period of time, physical deterioration ensues. As the physical decline proceeds, the threat of immobilization and forced dependence increases. A man or woman accustomed to independence suddenly requires outside aid in what was once an easy task. Fear of disability and the need for independence and self-mastery combine to produce strong anxiety in the dying patient.

In an emergency situation, we hope our actions will be appropriate and not under the control of intense emotion. In the same sense, we hope to maintain composure and cope with the very strong feelings that accompany the process of dying. The fear that we will not be able to cope with these emotions is derived in part from the fear of abandonment: if the dying patient becomes too emotional, maybe this will drive others away.

Dying is a new experience each time it happens because no one is allowed a repeat performance. Like death itself, the dying process is a big unknown to all who have not experienced it. Not knowing what to expect next, we envision the dying process to be full of "unpleasant surprises."[2] Knowledge of the illness involved is the best way to make the unknown known. Dying patients have the right to question their doctors about the nature of their illness, and physicians are duty-bound to answer to the best of their knowledge.

The fear of the dying process is composed of many related fears: abandonment, pain, loss of independence, emotional upset, and the unknown. With such fears associated with the death process, it is no wonder many people admit to fearing dying more than death.

Thus far we have defined death anxiety in different terms. Only a few of the multitude of individual fears were mentioned, and already the definition is complicated. Analyzing the origin of the fear of death is even more complex; many factors determine what one fears and to what extent. In addition, the analysis of death anxiety is confounded by our inability to distinguish cause from effect (the chicken-egg dilemma). Nevertheless, we can narrow the explanation of origin to two general headings: fear derived innately and fear derived through social interaction.

Death Anxiety Is Innate

A very substantial proportion of scholars consider "the fear of death to be virtually universal, or so prevalent as to be taken as universal."[3] Whether we examine an African culture or an industrialized Western society, one thing is obvious: nearly every human being fears death. The universality of the fear is the single most persuasive argument in favor of its innate origin. Why should so many different societies, which differ in so many other respects, be so similar when it comes to death anxiety?

Animals exhibit specific behavior in a dangerous situation. They are unable to conceive of death in human terms; they don't have the capacity to understand this abstract concept (which is not to imply that we completely understand death ourselves). And yet all animals with a true nervous system possess reflexes that assist in self-preservation. Dogs will bite when in danger, cats will scratch, and deer will run. Surely, human beings must possess at least a remnant of this instinct to survive. We remove our hand from a hot stove without being taught. The crying behavior of infants in response to strangers may be a self-preservation reflex.[4] Most will agree that humans are born with the instinct for self-preservation, but some insist it doesn't necessarily mean we are born with a fear of death. This is true; however, the survival instinct acts as a foundation upon which development of the death anxiety may commence. If we had no instinct to survive, death would no longer be feared. In this respect, the basic framework of the fear of death is innate in origin.

Many ancient societies feared the dead more than they feared death itself. Since the fear of the dead is merely an element of death anxiety, we can conclude that these ancient people did in fact fear death. The ancient Hebrews regarded the body of a dead person as something unclean and not to be touched. Early American Indians talked about evil spirits and shot arrows into the air to drive them away after the death of a member of the tribe. The tombstone may have originated as a device to keep the bad spirits deep in the ground. Very different in basic social life styles, the similarity of these fears points to a common fear of death. In general, even though societies may differ in the way they express their death anxiety, the fact that the fear is present leads us to theorize an innate, common origin.

In an experiment designed to measure relative fears of death at various levels, it was found that mentally disturbed persons (i.e., those with personality disorders) did not exhibit a greater fear of death than did normal subjects.[5] These results were in opposition to the anticipated outcome in which the mentally disturbed persons were expected to fear death in proportion to the degree of emotional disturbance. At least in this case, the fear of death remained constant, although the personalities of subjects differed greatly. We must not be too quick to infer the innate nature of death anxiety from these studies, however, because the subjects' similar environments might explain the similarities in the acquisition of death anxiety.

Verifying the innate nature of death fear is extremely difficult. A true scientific experiment would make use of a control, that is, an infant who had no social interaction and, therefore, no opportunity to be externally influenced. We could then measure the acquisition of the fear of death. First of all, no such control exists. Second, the control may possess a sense of self-preservation, but unless taught the abstract meaning of death through experience, the infant would never be able to develop a fear of death and would be little more than an animal. This would neither prove nor disprove the theory of innate acquisition since the child's entire functioning has been disrupted. If the child could be taught what death was (in completely neutral terms) with no social interaction whatsoever, this "self-taught" fear could be studied and the relative importance of social interaction to death fear acquisition could be evaluated. Since no such control will ever exist, we are left to infer from more indirect experiments. Therefore, to infer from the universality of the death fear that the origin of death anxiety has an innate component is somewhat dangerous. And yet to disprove its existence is just as difficult.

Death Anxiety is Modified After Birth

There is little doubt that the fear of death is affected by the society in which one lives. Pinpointing specific influences upon the incorporation of that fear is difficult, however. When comparing the impact of a particular experience on the development of an organism, we must remember that there are a multitude of other variables that may make analysis impossible. Second, the chicken-egg dilemma looms over us: for example, if farmers feared death more would it be because they were farmers, or did they decide to be farmers because they feared death more? Nevertheless, through experiments and hypotheses we can infer the modifying ability of a culture to influence the particularity and intensity of death anxiety.

Since we, as human beings, are fundamentally animals, we possess built-in instincts. However, we differ from all other animals in our conscious will; we have the power to make intelligent decisions after carefully considering the consequences of past actions.[6] This may be defined as "learning." Only we can learn the concept of death, an accomplishment achieved through our innate intelligence and modified by the environment in which we live. The number of environmental factors is infinite; the nature of a few of these factors will be discussed.

A correlation between fear of failure and fear of death has been hypothesized. Those with a great fear of personal failure often have an elevated fear of death.[7] Failure is the inability to attain ideal goals; death is an infringement that denies us the chance to attain those ideal goals. It is understandable that such a correlation exists between the two fears. A more general observation maintains that satisfaction with one's accomplishments in life decreases the fear of death. Those "in love" with life are less afraid than those who simply live life without stopping to smell the flowers. The way in which people perceive themselves is definitely affected by their environment and ultimately reflected in their attitude toward death.

The impact of religion on an individual is contradictory. Studies find that religion either increases or decreases the fear of death. Different religions meet the needs of an individual in different ways.

However, it appears the more strongly people believe in an after-life, the smaller their death anxiety. Perhaps this explains why Catholics, in general, fear death less than Protestants, who in turn fear it less than Jews.[8] It may also be plausible to expect those who fear punishment after death (hell) to fear death more. Since religion means different things to those within the same faith, we run into a problem when we believe "religious belief" to be an all-encompass-ing term. Basically, though, those who profess to be the most "reli-gious" fear death the least. Cases in which religion seems to increase the fear of death might occur because the more fearful persons choose to be more religious in an attempt to assuage their uneasi-ness. Analysis of the finding that the more religious are less afraid of death suggests a common effect of religion. Although they differ in certain ideals and beliefs, most religions do develop from a similar framework. Religion is generally believed to transcend death through a belief in some type of eternal life. Religion, then, might be described as a modifier of death anxiety.

Females tend to be more afraid of death and its connotations than males.[9] Although possibly genetically determined, a more reason-able explanation would include the effect of different social rearing. Boys are taught at an early age that fear is cowardly. Girls, on the other hand, are freer to express their emotions in our society and, therefore, appear to have increased general anxiety; females are not instilled as strongly with the notion that fear is for cowards. An ele-vated level of general anxiety might explain the elevated level of the dread of death. In such a case, the attitude and behavior of indivi-duals may be modified by the specific social rearing they receive.

Contradictory results have been obtained with regard to age dif-ferences. As an experiment, the subjects' fear of death was mea-sured on three levels: the conscious, imagery, and the subconscious. In most cases, the differences between age groups was small.[10] How-ever, the elderly denied the fear of death on a conscious level more than the young, although they fear death more on an unconscious level.[11] Closer to death, the elderly both fear and deny death more than the young; specifically, they have an increased aversion to the dying process.[12] Again, a small yet significant variation was recorded between middle-aged people (forty to sixty years) and all others. The middle-aged person appears to fear the death event more than the younger person and the older individual.[13] The young contemplate death little, the old are often more accustomed to the ever-present threat of death (although they may fear dying more). The stable and secure life of the middle-aged person suddenly is threatened by increasing age and approaching death. This realization leads to the rise in death anxiety.

Many other environmental factors that do not seem to affect the death fear have been studied. These elements include intelligence, socioeconomic status, marital status, number of children, and education.[14] Not every aspect of one's environment changes the death anxiety equally.

Soldiers in constant fear for their lives have a high level of anxiety. We might conclude, then, that exposure to death increases fear. This would explain why physicians fear death more than normal (although they think about it less).[15] The two groups are different, however. Soldiers are often drafted and so may not choose to fight; on the other hand, doctors practice because they so desire. We do not know for certain, then, whether physicians' exposure to death increases their fear, or whether they became doctors to cope with their already-present fear of death. Although we can argue that increased probability of one's death may tend to increase anxiety, it is difficult to conclude that mere exposure to death elevates fear. As a matter of fact, it seems that a recent exposure to death produces no substantial increase in death anxiety.[16]

The fear of death is a very complex thing. We have discussed some of the ways in which the anxiety of death can be modified by social and environmental factors: fear of failure (in a success-oriented society), religion, sex, age, and high probability of one's own death. This list is by no means complete.

The fear of death originates in an innate and embryonic form. Modified by experience, the embryonic fear develops the intensity and particularities we associate with the complex death anxiety.

Since the early years are the most important in terms of attitude development, observations of the first few years of life may lead us to a better understanding of the initial effects of environment on death fear.

Early Life: First Exposure to the Environment

Although the idea is somewhat farfetched, some psychologists believe the trauma of birth, the entrance into a hostile environment, may be the first step in the maturation process of the death anxiety. Studies indicate a possible correlation between a prolonged, intense parturition and greater instinctual fear.[17] From the first moment of life (and maybe while in the uterus), children must fight to survive. As infants, they are helpless and rely totally on others, especially their mother. Some contend this early fear of helplessness will carry over into the adult death anxiety.[18] As children grow they will be separated from their mother more and more. Perhaps this is the beginning of the fear of separation, which grows to a fear of death (separation). As earlier noted, the fear of death may be associated with a fear of punishment, instilled by the parents at an early age.

Children seek their mother's love as a safeguard against injury, pain, and death. The mother is a source of satisfaction and security. Infants fear abandonment by their mother and loss of this security. Loss of parents' love, then, becomes allied to loss of life; infants fear the loss of love (abandonment), which is later generalized to include fear of death and dying.

We have speculated about the relation of psychological development to the development of the fear of death. These are purely hypothetical. Let us now view the intellectual progression of children in terms of development of death attitudes.

There is a developmental stage in which speech is fairly well advanced and children don't understand death at all. This stage might be likened to the immature fear of death. Before the concept of death is understood by children, they must be able to organize experiences at a certain level and have reached some apprehension of causation. The point at which these two requirements are met is called the "why" stage. It is at this stage that children are strongly influenced by social teaching. Able to understand that a cause will produce an effect, questions about death begin to arise that the parents must answer. Children see dead animals and plants and ask why and how things die. Until they have reached this stage, death is not truly feared—they had no previous concept of its design. However, after this stage they sense the uneasiness with which parents discuss death. They learn to equate death with the effects of old age, and soon thoughts about their mother's death arouse anxiety in them.[19] Learning repression of fears is socially required. Children find themselves in a bind; they begin to fear death and yet have no outlet. The fear slowly builds within them as they reach adulthood. In general, we notice the prevalence of social influence quite early in the psychological and intellectual development of children. The origin of the fear of death does indeed have a cultural-environmental component that begins early in life when a person is most easily influenced.

The fear of death is not an evil to be eradicated, but a virtue that renders service to life. With no fear of death, we would not protect ourselves by building shelters, curing diseases, and implementing traffic laws. Death is a real, omnipresent danger, and fear of such a real threat is completely rational. The ubiquitous existence of death anxiety for so many years supports the view that the fear is an evolutionary adaptation.

If the death fear is innate and universal, then why do we feel uncomfortable to admit we have this fear? In our society fear is often associated with immaturity and weakness; it is to be overcome, not cultivated. From the earliest years of life we learn to repress our anxieties, to cover them up, to pretend they do not exist; but denying the presence of a rational, innate, and socially imprinted death fear can be dangerous. The result is a fear of the fear of death, which is irrational yet devastating. The increased denial of fear in America today may have developed as a protective measure. We have broadened our understanding of nearly every other natural enigma: we know much about the universe from space travel and the telescope;

we know much about the atomic universe from physics, chemistry, and the microscope. However, we have not increased our knowledge of death one iota—we haven't been able to define the precise moment of death, let alone what it means to be dead. We deny that we fear death in order to overcome its power—we will not let it get the best of us. Such attempts are futile, though, since we still fear death, but in a repressed form.

The advance of technology has influenced our fear of death in another way. The mortality rate has declined in recent years and people live to be older on the average. In the past, young children were exposed to death in the nuclear family, in general, at a much younger age. There were more orphans in past years.[20] Today, more of us have not experienced the death of a loved one. Unfamiliarity with death lets us ignore it and repress our fears. Although those exposed to death early may not fear it less than others, they are not as prone to repress their fear.

> There are various ways of attempting to cope with the fear of death. We may try to ignore it; we never mention it, and always attempt to turn our thoughts in another direction when we find ourselves dwelling on it . . . . Or we may adopt the exactly opposite course and meditate continually on the brevity of human life in the hope that familiarity will breed contempt.[21]

Ideally, the way we should cope with death lies somewhere between these two extremes. We can't think about death continually; how, then, would we enjoy life? Avoiding the thought of death completely, we may be confronted unexpectedly with the harsh reality of our own mortality. Perhaps the realization of our own death fears, whether rational or irrational, will alleviate the pressure and anxiety associated with the death of a loved one, and will eventually allow us to accept our own death with reduced anxiety and increased equanimity.

2

To Tell or not to Tell

> *To every thing there is a season, and a time to*
> *   every purpose under heaven:*
> *a time to be born, and a time to die; a time to plant,*
> *   and a time to pluck up that which is planted;*
> *a time to kill, and a time to heal; a time to*
> *   break down, and a time to build up;*
> *a time to weep, and a time to laugh; a time to mourn,*
> *   and a time to dance;*
> *a time to cast away stones, and a time to gather stones*
> *   together; a time to embrace, and a time to*
> *   refrain from embracing;*
> *a time to get, and a time to lose; a time to keep, and*
> *   a time to cast away;*
> *a time to rend, a time to sew; a time to keep silence,*
> *   and a time to speak;*
> *a time to love, and a time to hate; a time of war, and*
> *   a time of peace.*
>
> —Book of Ecclesiastes

In our society death is viewed as a failure, a catastrophe, an unnatural or immoral act we should be shielded from. This attitude is an expected response to our medical technological "progress." The dying process can now be unnecessarily extended; it is increasingly mechanical and fearfully dehumanizing. But instead of working to combat such fears, most physicians tend to reinforce and promote them by refusing to accept the fact that there is a time to die.

Cancer is a very difficult disease for physicians to deal with, both medically and emotionally. Physicians feel helpless and resourceless in that they have no means for controlling or curing this slow, pitiful deterioration of the human body. Consequently, to avoid failure, physicians will avoid honest and direct contact with the dying cancer patient. However, the quality of the physician-patient relationship is of the utmost importance. This relationship, from the onset, should be based on mutual trust and respect. Unfortunately, this trust is impossible to establish in cases where a diagnosis of malignancy is made and the physician decides to withhold the truth. Physicians fail, then, not in that they cannot cure, but in that they deny their dying patients a time for gathering stones together; a time to embrace; a time to get; a time to lose; and most important, a time to die.

Physicians owe their patients the truth fully and honestly; the facts about a patient's health are only entrusted to the physician—they belong to the patient. The most important reason for being honest with a patient is to maintain that relationship of mutual trust between physician and patient. Withholding information jeopardizes this personal relationship and thereby jeopardizes the fullest possibilities of emotional care and medical treatment, since they both depend on respect and confidence, as well as technical skill. Once the truth has been told with compassion, and trust and candor between the physician and patient have been established, subsequent discussions become easier. Clearly and simply, without rationalizations and unnecessary apologies, patients can be told about new symptoms and why older symptoms have not responded to treatment. Patients need to be told that they will have enough medication to reduce pain. Parents and older children need to know when procedures that merely prolong survival are being considered.

Dying patients usually have fairly good insight into their condition, and to many patients the anxiety of not knowing their real diagnosis must be at least as great as knowing the truth—if it is told in a compassionate and humane manner. As patients' questions about treatment, medication, and symptoms go unanswered, their despair and frustration may intensify. These patients lose all hope because they feel their prognosis is so terrible that even the physician won't mention it.

It is difficult to determine the number of patients who know the truth without ever being told. In one study, Thomas Hackett undertook psychotherapy of twenty patients who were dying of cancer, but had not been told about the diagnosis of cancer or the imminence of their death. During the interviews, all twenty revealed that they knew they were dying, probably of cancer, and that the facts were being withheld from them. When asked why they remained silent about their discovery, the patients usually said that they assumed the doctor and other family members did not want to talk with them about their disease. They joined the conspiracy of silence in order to protect the doctor and their families from the discomfort and the difficulty of talking about an unpleasant problem.[22]

Withholding the truth from patients will result in their isolation from people who care because of their assigned roles and the image that their condition is not critical. Their sources of comfort, hope, and love are lost in this charade, and they usually live and die in isolation and loneliness.

Once the initial shock that comes with confirming the dying patients' belief is over, the patients are then given the freedom of choice (or knowledge) over their own body, their medication, and their plans for their remaining days. In many ways this can be a relaxing process—patients can cease struggling with the world about them, they can take time to do things for themselves and for their loved ones, they can share things that had up to then been left unsaid, and loved ones can share with them.

Physicians cannot assume the life-and-death responsibilities of patients, for patients alone know their own obligations and specific responsibilities that need handling. If patients are not told of approaching death, or at least of its grave possibility, they may fail to make proper preparation in wills and testaments, or in reparations and restorations of one kind or another, or in reconciliations with God and/or men.[23]

Also, without the truth, some adult patients may refuse costly forms of treatment, since the urgency is not apparent to them. Some years ago the Division of Cancer of the Massachusetts Department of Public Health issued a bulletin in which it was noted that patients who were told frankly about their disease were fully cooperative about treatment. On the other hand, some patients who do undergo decisive forms of treatment, surgical or otherwise, may have objected to it if they had known their true prognosis.

Although our concern should be centered around the patient, a study by Dr. Colin Parks indicates that not only is preparation for death beneficial to the patient, but it is beneficial to the survivors.

> . . . Of 68 young American widows and widowers who were interviewed at intervals after bereavement, there were 24 who had had little advance warning that their husbands or wives were going to die. Their reaction to bereavement was much more severe and prolonged than those who had had adequate warning. Even two, three or four years later these men and women were significantly more depressed, more anxious, self-reproaching and coping less well with financial and other responsibilities than those who had had at least two weeks warning that death was likely to occur and at least three days' warning that it was imminent. It seems therefore, that advance warning of an approaching death is important to the mental health of the survivors.[24]

Physicians and patients differ dramatically when asked what should be told to a terminally ill patient. In a study by Fitts and Ravdin, 444 Philadelphia physicians were questioned about what they told patients with cancer. Eighty-nine percent of the physicians responded; of these, 3 percent always tell the patient, 28 percent usually tell, 57 percent usually do not tell, and 12 percent never tell. Some physicians included additional comments on the questionnaire to substantiate their views. One declared: "It is bad enough to have cancer, and the physician should not rob the patient of what little pleasure may be left in life for him. I can see at no time any reason why the patient should know he has cancer. The dread of the return of the disease, even if the patient is cured, is horrible."

Another stated: "I feel strongly against letting the patient know he has cancer! To all people, intelligent or not, the word cancer means a death sentence, and even if you meet an occasional patient who insists on knowing the worst and says that it will not affect him one way or another, he will be mentally affected by knowing the worst."

Another physician, however, seemed to have a different point of view:

> I always tell the patient he has cancer. In forty years I had only two instances where the full truth was not well received. You can create distrust in the profession or bitter loss of faith in the family if deception is practiced by anyone. All patients can bravely face even death if they know the truth and trust the honesty of the one they have selected to aid. They condemn their physician or even their close family if they discover they have been deceived and will not even trust a favorable prognosis should such be possible. To deceive a patient or even evade a real fact of certain death, is to torture the intelligence of those who will know, even if it be at the very last, that they could trust no one.[25]

A second study shows even more physicians withholding the truth from their patients. Questionnaires and interviews were used to study the information disclosing policies of 219 physicians affiliated with a major hospital in Chicago. Eighty-eight percent of the physicians do not tell their patients of a cancer diagnosis, and therefore only 12 percent usually do tell.

The data from studies asking patients what should be told to someone with a terminal illness are remarkably different from the studies of physician responses. Kelly and Friesen surveyed two groups of patients, each group consisting of one-hundred cases. The first group consisted of patients who had established cancer diagnoses, while the other group were noncancer patients. In the first group, eighty-nine said they preferred to know about the cancer, six said they would rather not have known, five were indefinite; whereas in the second group eighty-two said they would want to be told, fourteen said they do not want to be told, and four were indefinite. It is interesting to note that although eighty-nine cancer patients preferred to know about the cancer with respect to themselves, only seventy-three cancer patients thought that patients in general should be informed. The logic that others are not quite as capable to accept the truth as oneself is again at work here, as it is with several physicians. Kelly and Friesen also questioned another group of 740 people being examined at a cancer detection center. (These patients were apparently well; they underwent these medical examinations in an effort to detect cancer at an early stage.) Of these, 729 (98.5 percent) wanted to be told, 7 (.9 percent) did not, and 4 (.5 percent) were indefinite.[26]

Yet, another study carried out by Samp and Curreri found patients consistently reporting that they would like to be told. They asked patients and visitors in a waiting room of a tumor clinic: "If a patient has cancer, should he or she be told of this fact?" Of the 560 people asked, 451 (81 percent) answered yes unequivocally, 62 (11 percent) answered no unequivocally, and 47 (8 percent) needed to qualify their responses.[27]

Why do such discrepancies between what patients need to know and what physicians disclose exist? Various reasons for withholding terminal diagnoses are offered to us by physicians. Although motives seem genuine, a closer examination of them can lead us to question who is protecting whom, who is sparing whom.

Some physicians feel that informing patients of their true diagnosis is tantamount to sentencing them to death. However, does withholding the information make cancer any less of a reality? For the patient, certainly not; for the physician, it definitely does. It would appear that since patients need and benefit from knowing the truth, the evasion of the truth is a protective mechanism for physicians; it is a denial of their helplessness and a rationalization of their own embarrassment. Many physicians will say they can sense that a certain patient is not emotionally prepared to hear the truth. Dr. Kübler-Ross raises some serious problems about the ability of physicians to sense denial in their patients. "I am convinced from the many patients with whom I have spoken about this matter, that those doctors who need denial themselves will find it in their patients and that those who can talk about the terminal illness will find their patients better able to face and acknowledge it. The need of denial is in direct proportion with the doctor's need for denial."[28]

Another rationalization used by physicians is the fear that suicide will follow a terminal diagnosis. Studies, however, have shown that suicides rarely occur following the acknowledgment of cancer. Litin found that out of all the suicides committed in Rochester, Minnesota, over a ten-year period, there was only one case with any temporal relationship to the person being told he had cancer.[29] Dr. Walter Alvarez of the Mayo Clinic said, " . . . Often it is the relatives who have fear and mental pain. . . . In forty-odd years of practice I cannot remember anyone committing suicide because I told him the hopeless truth. Instead, hundreds of persons thanked me from their hearts and told me I had relieved their minds." People *do* want to live out their lives to the fullest—be it ten years or ten weeks. Once the realization of the finiteness of life is accepted, we are liberated to enjoy each and every day as we see fit.

Some physicians feel that the lack of complete certainty excuses them from any obligation to tell the truth. This argument, however, is clearly not valid. If, in fact, there is uncertainty in the diagnosis, then this should be communicated to the patient. Quite often the boundaries of uncertainty are broadened so that the physician can hide his responsibilities behind this facade.

A provocative study carried out by Herman Feifel and his colleagues measured the fear of death of physicians and of healthy and seriously (some terminally) ill patients. A forty-item questionnaire was used and all the responses were coded independently by two of the investigators, all of whom held diplomas in clinical psychology and psychiatry. The results indicated that the physicians were significantly more afraid of death than either the healthy or sick lay people. It is sadly ironic that this above-average fear of death is seemingly a factor in the physician's selection of medicine as a career and also a great hindrance when dealing with something common to all patients—death.

Withholding the truth from a patient seems to be aimed at satisfying the needs, emotional and otherwise, of the physician, rather than those of the patient. For it is clear that a physician's decision not to tell does not mean the patient will not find out; it does mean, however, that when the patient does come to learn the prognosis, then all trust is irrevocably destroyed. And there are so many other ways a patient can find out about this condition even if physician, family, and friends avoid the topic. Patients can observe changes in staff behavior, increased or decreased attention, solicitous concern from someone who was formerly matter-of-fact, serious facial expressions, consultations in the corridor, whispering, withdrawal of some, and saddened faces of relatives. All are signals by which patients guess at their prognosis.

Unfortunately, today we see that most patients have a double attitude toward doctors—one of respect and trust but also of suspicion that doctors are withholding information (to some degree). Doctors are not only undermining patient confidence in themselves, but they are making medical practice a manipulation of bodies rather than a caring for individuals. A good example of lack of trust in physicians was found in the newspapers of February 1923. The prizefighter J. J. Corbett had died of cancer, and the *New York Times* ran the story with this headline: "Ex-Champion Succumbs Here to Cancer. He Believed He Had Heart Disease." Such was the conscientious lie with which Corbett's doctor had let him live out his last days. Soon however, doctors began to protest violently the publication of this deception in a news story. One physician complained to the editor that several of his patients with heart disease were wild with fear that they too had cancer of the liver.[30]

Clearly, for the benefit of all concerned, physicians must be able to admit to and accept their own limitations without shame or self-recrimination. It is understandable that continual confrontation with dying patients may lead the physician to avoid exposure to cancer patients and to maintain a professional distance. However, dealing with the dying is a major part of being a caring and competent physician, and it is an area in which many doctors need to improve. Rationalizing that the patient would be better off not knowing will no longer do—it is an avoidance of responsibility.

Dr. Kübler-Ross has often said that the question is not "Should we tell?" but rather "How do I share this with my patient?" Telling patients the truth about their terminal illness involves tremendous emotional interplay and upheaval. How to share the information is a difficult decision because of the varying personalities of physician and patient. It is most important that a relationship of mutual trust and respect be established between doctor and patient. With this relationship intact, the impersonal, short-term, and callous qualities of the hospital setting can be overcome. Just as conscientious physicians try to benefit, and not harm, with drug or knife, so they also treat with their words and their expressions of feeling. Physicians' expressions of concern for their patients (of any age), their establishment of the link of humanity between them, is healing no matter what the prognosis.

Physicians must be able to create an atmosphere where anxieties can be minimized. They should initiate discussions with patients to get at their feelings, fears, needs, and desires. They must bear in mind that the patients' main concerns at this time include fear of isolation and abandonment, fear of intractable pain, fear of institutional care—and the doctor must be sure to address these fears. Also, this is not and cannot be a "one-shot" venture. Time is necessary for any such exchange, and physicians must be sensitive to how much should be told at any one moment. They should create a setting in which patients are able to come to terms with their situation, in their own time.

An ideal physician should be humane, gentle, understanding and consistently constructive in his selection of facts and words for the purpose of communicating usable knowledge about cancer to both the patient and the family. He should not be unduly pessimistic or optimistic. He should hold out no false hope, yet be careful to verbalize clearly every fact which lends hope. There must be time available for the telling and for the discussions which follow.[31]

A classic case of how *not* to deal with the problem of disclosure was reported by Glaser and Strauss.[32] They described the practice of one hospital, which informed patients who had fatal illnesses in short, blunt announcements. As would be expected, sociologists studying this treatment mode found that it simply amplified depression and despair. In this hospital, telling the patient was looked at as an end unto itself, as a painful task to be gotten out of the way, or to be relinquished gladly to someone else.

Patients, because of their individuality, will react very differently to a careful and caring explanation of their condition. Patients will each react according to their personalities, influenced by their past experiences and previous beliefs. Some will face the truth with great courage and equanimity, and in some cases young children will show a maturity far beyond their years. Others may refuse to accept the news (at least for the time being), while others may feel despair or depression.

Physicians should be prepared for any reaction. From it, they can learn a great deal about the very special needs of their patients and how to meet them. Physicians must realize that the immediate coping with such news is intensely painful and time-consuming. Preparing oneself to die takes time—a time for denial, a time for anger, a time for bargaining, a time for depression, and one hopes, also a time for acceptance. For both doctor and patient this time allows for a precious process whereby a quality of intimacy reaffirms a vital relationship. For if physicians can both "speak the truth in love" (Eph. 4:15) and listen to their patients in love, they can rest assured that their patients will have a tranquil terminal period.

What about those patients who request not to be told anything? It appears that they realize the severity of their prognosis, but yet, they cannot bear to be told about it. They are probably functioning under the assumption that a physician with promising news would definitely override their wishes. Conversely, if the prognosis were poor, the physician would avoid such a discussion. Although forcing the truth upon patients is not advisable, physicians should explain why they feel the patient should know. In this discussion, even if patients continue to resist the truth, the doctor should try to alleviate their fears of abandonment, isolation, and pain. One must recognize that a patient may require time to face a catastrophic threat of this kind. A consistently supportive and encouraging attitude on the part of the physician may, over a period of time, make it possible for the patient to face this painful information.

Dr. Raphael Ginzberg believes that death has a very different significance for elderly patients. Death is no longer a remote possibility; it is a reality that awaits them. He concludes however, that "the sick elderly person who knows that his condition is hopeless is therefore more profoundly disturbed. His hopelessness is more firmly fixed than in the younger patient, and the psychological reaction to pain, weakness, and other organic changes is much more outspoken. Exhaustion and pain especially are constant reminders that there is no way back to life."[33] It is clear that persons of any age will react to the disclosure of the fact that they are hopelessly ill. However, this reaction should not excuse physicians from discussing the patients' condition with them. Clearly, doctors should not speak of a quantified period of time left, but should gently and compassionately explain, for example, what symptoms should be expected, how they will be relieved, what treatment will be necessary. Although Ginzberg's contention that elderly patients have considered their own death more fully than younger patients is accurate, this realization of one's finiteness should not act as an obstacle in the path of honesty. Many opportunities for sharing wisdom, maturity, and love are wasted because we deny our elderly patients the truth. The elderly are often very lonely people, thought of as outcasts of society. We cannot allow them the continued abandonment of dying in isolation and deception.

On the other end of life's spectrum we find another group of individuals "in need of protection"—children. Considerable effort is often expended to keep a diagnosis of terminal cancer a secret from children. However, no matter how hard their parents and physicians may try, children quickly sense that something is seriously wrong. This may even lead to behavioral problems in that they can no longer rely on the persons they had come to trust and love.

> Upon admission to the hospital, patient E, age 10, was extremely apprehensive, uncooperative, and withdrawn, and he consistently whined and cried. He refused to take his medications. During interviews with p;atient E, it was learned that he did not know his diagnosis. He went on to say that while he had been in the office of his family physician, his parents were called out of the room and he was left alone. He was never told what they had discussed, but he knew that his parents had knowledge which had not been shared with him, and he was extremely worried about what had been said.... After [some convincing]...his parents gave his doctor permission to speak with the child about his diagnosis. This disclosure paved the way for the ward staff to help patient E come to grips with his situation in a completely open fashion. His behavior took a remarkable change for the better. He became cheerful and relaxed and the problem of his refusing medications all but disappeared.[34]

Dying children, like dying adults, also worry and fear the dying process. They are eager and relieved to have someone to talk with and to answer their questions. Physicians should create an environment where children feel free to ask any question and feel secure that they are getting an honest response.

Telling fellow human beings that they have a terminal disease such as cancer is very difficult. However, it is clear that only harm is inflicted by withholding information. And yet, because our society is so afraid of death, physicians still continue to disguise the truth. Perhaps we should begin by teaching the truth about death and dying to people of all ages. The realization that death is but a continuation of life should be taught along with other aspects of life. If we allow the dying to return to their place in their homes, to return from mechanization and impersonalization, and to be considered living human beings, we will find that they have much wisdom and love to share with us. We would cherish these opportunities always.

> No one better than a dying patient will help us to come to peace with our own finiteness. If we spend a little time with them, if we can hear them when they are ready to talk, they will teach us not only what it is like to be dying, but also essential lessons in living. It is their gift to us for taking a little time out of our rushed schedules when their values begin to change to the real values of life. The real values we often discover too late—unless we listen to our dying patients.
>
> —Elisabeth Kübler-Ross

3

The Child Discovers Death

Children's reactions to death are related to a variety of factors. Among these are the attitudes of parents and other adults in their environment, their relation to the object loss, their stage of psychological development, the circumstances of loss, previous exposure to death, and religious concepts. In this chapter I will focus on children's responses to death loss and the influence that the above factors may have on their capacity for mourning and grieving.

Some authorities have said that Americans have a cultural inability to face death. Kübler-Ross has pointed out that death is viewed as a taboo, discussion of it is regarded as morbid, and children are excluded from being near the dead and dying, with the presumption and pretext that it would be "too much for them."

Because of the anxiety about death that adults harbor, they have a strong tendency to shield a child from death and dying. Death cannot be hidden from children. The parent who tries to protect a child from the experience of death is only adding confusion and anxiety to an already difficult world. When someone in a family is dying or has died, the feelings of the adult family members are transmitted to children by many nonverbal clues such as facial expression, tone of voice, and body posture.

Most wise parents realize that children should not be excluded from sharing grief and sorrow any more than they should be from sharing joy and happiness in the course of normal family relationships. When a death occurs, and children are not told exactly what has happened, they may become confused and feel great anxiety.

They may fill their knowledge gap with figments of their imagination, which may be much more frightening to them than the truth could ever be.

In discussing death as a strong taboo in our culture, Nelson and Peterson state that lack of death education contributes to misunderstanding, fear, and an unpreparedness for a reality of life. With each succeeding year of life, it becomes more likely that young persons will encounter death in a direct and personal way. They may have experienced the death of a grandparent, a parent, or a sibling. They may have also been exposed to the death of national figures. Most young people have also experienced the loss of a pet, which can be as upsetting to them as the death of a human.

Regardless of whether they have or have not experienced the death of someone of personal significance, young people have encountered both the realities and unrealities of death as presented by television. Cartoons, comic books, and literature often present torture and death.

Although the experiences young people have with death may leave them quite capable of facing death, they may also be left with warped and distorted views. It is important that they be given more than the fears and silence of adults in relation to the topic of death.

The question arises constantly about what we should tell a child when death occurs. Should we avoid acknowledgment that the person has died? Should we say that the lost has "gone away"? Should we suggest that the person became ill and had to go to a hospital, in the hope that the child's memory of this person would fade away and the child would eventually accept this absence as normal? All these evasions merely indicate the uncertainty the adult has about the child's capacity to deal with reality situations.

It is possible to explain to a child the process of growing up and dying as one sees it repeated in flowers, trees, and as a phenomenon that occurs throughout nature. The child is able to grasp this concept and to recognize that the same process occurs in animals and in human beings. The manner in which the adult presents the facts determines how the child will accept the explanation.

The easiest way for a parent to explain the death of a relative to a young child is through the use of euphemisms. Hendin feels such simplistic talk should be avoided. Even though many have the feeling that a half-truth will upset a child less than facts, few children older than two actually believe such white lies. Hendin gives an example of a four-year-old who, told that her grandfather had "gone to his eternal sleep," asked whether he had taken his pajamas with him. In considering such an explanation, her parents should have realized that the child herself had to go to sleep every night. Such an explanation can result in severe anxiety.

Religious training influences what the child will learn about death and afterlife. Religions do differ in what they teach. Children exposed to death in a nonfrightening way tend to be less fearful of death. Those who believe in a benevolent God and reunion after death may be more hopeful than those who believe the opposite. Even parents who do not espouse organized religion and beliefs may encourage their children to retain belief in God when learning about death. Gorer, in his survey of British parents, made some interesting points in regard to the use of religious euphemisms by parents in explaining death to their children. The most prevalent of the religious euphemisms are "gone to heaven," "gone to Jesus," and the like. What is noteworthy, Gorer states, is that these religious euphemisms are frequently used by people who seem to have no religious convictions themselves. It appears a sizable minority of British parents are using God and Jesus in communicating with their children exactly the same way they use Santa Claus—as fairy-tale figures.[35]

The development of a concept of death takes place by stages that are directly related to the normal developmental sequence of biological and psychological growth. Age influences children's ideas about death and these ideas influence the way they respond when they encounter death.

Researchers have been limited to observing behavior during the first two years of a child's life and guessing about its possible relevance to death because the child lacks language skills. Most experts agree, however, that the child of less than three years has no conception of death. The child may have been experimenting with a "preidea" of death in games of peek-a-boo and disappearance-and-return.[36] Children less than three years old do not distinguish between death and absence. They think of death as separation and may talk about dead people as though they are still living.

The majority of children between three and five years old begin to understand death as something that happens to others. They seek to isolate the phenomena that "mean" or cause death because they are increasingly aware that death is important and destructive. These children tend to personify death as a creature of the night. They may believe that those who die are carried off by a monster or other being. Whoever can get away does not die. These children's ideas about death are strongly affected by their feelings in response to reactions with their parents.[37]

Children who are five to nine years old begin to identify death as a personal event. They often conceive of death as an external agent and associate death with injury and mutilation.[38] Ten-year-olds seem to have made the transition in both mental development and emotional security; they express an understanding of death as a final and inevitable outcome of life.

Piaget suggests that, as children approach adolescence, they are equipped with most of the intelligence necessary to understand both life and death in a logical manner. They now have completed the basic development of concepts of time, space, quality, and causality. This gives them the framework within which the idea of death can be placed. As adolescents begin to make their own decisions, they become aware that all their hopes, expectations, and ambitions require time for their actualization. Some adolescents devote a good deal of thought to the subject of death. Many avoid a direct exploration of death but show great concern on a less direct, less conscious level.[39] Although they conceptualize death as an inevitable process, they may not comprehend death as an event occurring to a person close to them.

The stage of psychological development the child has reached at the time of a death loss is an important factor in his or her response to the loss. Wolfenstein described a child's reaction to the death of a parent as an inhibited emotional response and designated as "mourning at a distance" the apparent contradiction observed between the intensity of the grief shown for someone far away, as contrasted with mourning of a close relative. Wolfenstein believes that mourning becomes possible only with the resolution of the adolescent phase, after the appropriate detachment from the parental figures has taken place.

Many factors contribute to the specific forms of mourning reactions observed in children following the loss of important objects. These vary according to the different levels of development reached in a number of areas of the personality at different ages. In order to understand the reactions of children to loss, it is essential to examine the role that the object plays at different stages of the child's physical, psychological, and emotional development.

Rosenblatt explains that the term *object* in psychoanalysis refers primarily to persons rather than things. In regard to the child's reaction to death, the level of object relation achieved at the time of loss plays a large part in determining the subsequent reaction. According to Rosenblatt, in the first few months after birth, the baby's relations with objects is such that objects are interchangeable. In this early stage, the loss of a mother would not be catastrophic to the infant so long as another person were immediately available to take care of the baby's needs. The substitute mother might create a temporary discomfort for the child because she uses different methods of handling, but the loss of the mother as a person would not create this discomfort.

At about seven to nine months, most infants show a reaction to other faces known as "stranger anxiety." This fearful response to persons other than the mother indicates that the baby is beginning to discriminate between the mother and all others. Now the substitution of another person for a lost mother will have a different effect and the infant may show something like grief in response to the loss.

Rosenblatt further indicates that a child probably cannot react with true grief until another phase in the development of the object relations has been reached. This development is known as "object constancy," a phrase meant to describe the capacity to remember and represent an object in the mind even when the object is absent. This phase is reached at about fifteen to eighteen months. Until this level is achieved the loss of mother might create a serious disturbance in a child, with a sense of loss too global and too diffuse to be called grief and mourning. But after the level of object constancy is established and a picture of the mother has become an enduring mental representation in the mind, the possibility of grief, mourning, and depression in a more familiar form is also established with it. Not only the loss of mother, but the loss of any person in the intimate family circle could have powerful consequences for the surviving child.[40]

Nagera has slightly different views concerning the mourning process in children. He agrees more with Wolfenstein's view that mourning as observed in the adult is not possible until the adolescent stage. This does not imply that some aspects of the mourning process of the adult mourner cannot be observed in children, but Nagera sees important differences between the so-called mourning of children and that of adults. For the adult, as Nagera explains, the death of a close relative is frequently a traumatic event. For the child, the death of a close relative such as a mother or father is not only a traumatic event, but a serious developmental interference.[41]

The mourning that accompanies the loss of an object in adulthood is described as a process of adaptation. While the adaptation is worked through, everything else is temporarily suspended until the mourning is completed and the mourner resumes a normal life. But children are not finished products like adults. They are in the middle of a multiplicity of processes of development that require the presence of the suddenly absent object. This developmental need partly opposes the normal process of mourning and gradual withdrawal of cathexis from the lost object.

Another difference between the mourning reactions of children and those of adults is that children frequently react to the death of a primary object with abnormal manifestations, such as anxiety or multiple forms of regression, and by developing abnormal types of behavior. These reactions demonstrate the special situation of developmental stress in which children find themselves. Some children, for example, react to the parent's death with stealing and truancy. In normal adult mourning such a reaction is not usually observed.

We can observe some aspects of mourning in children as the meaningful psychological response to the loss of an object. In this respect it resembles such mourning responses of adults as protest, despair, and denial.

Several reactions have been observed to be typical in children's responses to death loss. In considering the reactions of children to the death of a parent or sibling, Wessel notes that there are always two issues. The first is to what degree children recognize the loss and can express their feelings of sadness and grief. The second is the question as to how far it is possible for children to mourn or to painfully withdraw their attachment to an adult who is no longer available as a person to whom they can attach their love.[42]

Denial is a defense used by children in traumatic or stressful situations. It is also a very common reaction of children to death loss. As Wessel points out, children of school age can be acutely aware of the reality of death and consequent physical disappearance of the person. Nevertheless, for their psychological growth they need to possess a mother or father. Children and adolescents, therefore, tend to keep the dead person very much alive in their minds. Often they appear to be able to discuss and accept death on one level of functioning, and simultaneously deny it on another level.[43]

At the moment a child is told of the death of a loved one, the child is likely to become pensive, sad, and weepy; but typically this lasts for a short time only. A few hours or days later, the child may ask to go to the movies or watch television. This "short sadness span" as Wolfenstein calls it, represents the limited capacity for tolerance of acute pain in children. Children in the age range from latency to adolescence cannot tolerate intense distress for long and quickly bring forward opposite thoughts and feelings. Children do not seem able to sustain the process of extended mourning that we know in adults. This may be a sort of protective denial, for if one feels good then nothing bad has happened. Perhaps the child protects himself with partial denial until he can assimilate the loss.

The phenomenon of demonstrable grief and what Wolfenstein called "mourning at a distance" is frequent in children. An interesting aspect of children's reactions to President Kennedy's death was that some seemed more openly upset than they had been at an earlier time when a close family member died. Wolfenstein's interpretation of this phenomenom is that, as meaningful and important as President Kennedy was, he was not a father to any but his own children. The loss, though upsetting to all, did not compare to the real loss of a parent. The grief at his assassination, though painful, was not as intolerable as what is experienced when having to give up a real parent.

A ten-year-old boy, for example, unable to cry at the time of his mother's death, began to sob intensely three months later while reading a story in which the main character died. A sad episode in a television program or the death of a goldfish will often be the occasion for releasing feelings that had been pent up since the death of a loved one.[44]

In order to understand why it is sometimes easier to express grief about a remote object than one closer to home, Wolfenstein explains that it is important to distinguish two aspects of reaction to loss. One is the release of sad feelings, the other giving up the lost object. Inhibited feelings press for outlet in one direction or another. At the same time, there is a strong objection against admitting that someone urgently needed is lost beyond call. If one begins to weep for the lost person, it is a step toward admitting the reality of the loss. But if one weeps by substitution for a remote object, feelings are released and at the same time denial of the loss can be maintained.

Guilt is another common reaction to death and plays an important role in grieving. As Howener and Phillips state, expressions of not having done enough while the person was alive or self-incrimination for failing to perform a saving act are frequently made by grieving adults. Similar guilt feelings are often present in young children in both death and divorce situations, but are related to children's thinking that their actions caused the person to die. Death-associated guilt often exists in young children because they are in a state of development when they believe they can cause events around them to happen.[45]

It is inevitable that young children will feel partially or fully responsible when they lose a parent or sibling. Most people, when young, during a moment of anger or frustration, wished their mother, father, brother, or sister to drop dead. These wishes to do away with a rival are known as death wishes. If a little boy wishes his mother would drop dead, and then she really does, the child will always feel that he actually killed her. Not only will he feel guilty, but he will also feel terribly deserted and frightened or angry. This child needs assurance that wishes do not and cannot kill.[46]

Hostile reactions resulting from the survivor's feelings of anger at being left and separated from the loved one are often a part of grieving. A child's despair at the loss of a loved one can lead to great anger. It is natural for a child, or any of us, to become angry when a prized possession is taken away. Anger may not be expressed openly by a bereaved child, but may be shown through misbehavior or more frequent fights in school. It is very important for a child to understand that, although the death was nobody's fault, it is normal to feel angry about it.

Fear is still another commonly observed reaction children have to death. Kalish tells us that children are more vulnerable to fear of dying for several reasons. Not understanding the nature of death or the causes of death, children are more likely to be confused by believing that death was a direct punishment for improper behavior, and they may worry that their naughty behavior will be similarly punished. Another not infrequent reaction of children is to direct anger, fear, or even hatred against God for producing the death. That death is the result of chance or of natural causes is incomprehensible to children, and they often have a need to understand death with someone or something as responsible.[47]

The death of a brother or sister causes the other children in the family to have fears about their own death. In general, parents can reassure them that they are well and that there is no reason to fear that they will die. However, this explanation is inadequate in those situations in which the disease that killed one child is present in other children in the family. In such cases, it is important that parents let the surviving children talk about their concern and that they tell them that doctors are constantly finding out more about the dead child's condition and may soon discover an effective treatment.

Robinson further notes that the reason for death is a concept that children have difficulty understanding. Like adults, they are puzzled by their feelings toward the deceased and are unwilling to accept the idea of a world in which death comes by chance to children. Children often believe that their parents were somehow responsible for the sibling's death and may also cause them to die. Although many parents are shocked by this, it is only by open expression of this notion that children can be reassured and can be able to cope with this fear.

Even if children are old enough to comprehend the finality of death, as Robinson states, they do not have the emotional resources of an adult. They may seem quite casual in their reaction to the death of a sibling because they must protect themselves from the full impact of their feelings of loss, guilt, and fear about their own death and that of their parents.

Children's fears are reinforced in our society because we don't express our true feelings when death occurs. Kalish tells us that modern middle-class children are likely to be as shielded from death as their counterparts of a century ago were shielded from human sexual behavior. Children's contact with the dying person is limited. Even discussions of the dying and death are conducted in whispers and stop abruptly when children enter the room. This behavior frightens children more, since they know something is going on and they have only the vaguest notion of what it is.

Zeligs agrees with Kalish's views in regard to children's fears and adult attitudes toward death. According to Zeligs, a great deal of children's fears and fantasies about death could be allayed if we did not make death a taboo subject but spoke of it freely and factually. This way children could satisfy their curiosity about what death is, the cause of the death of someone, and where people go when they die. But children sense the evasion and taboos against talking freely with their parents about the meaning of death.

The adults' attitudes toward death are absorbed by their children. Many adults have an unrealistic attitude toward the fact that human beings are mortal and will eventually die. They refuse to talk about death or face the fact that, sooner or later, they will die. But if parents can accept the reality of death and deal with it, children too can be less fearful. They can then have the expectations that their own death and that of their parents are probably a long way off. On the whole, children's reactions to an experience with death are greatly influenced by the way their parents and other authoritative figures conduct themselves during such an event.

Children's fears are enhanced when parents exclude children from experiences with death. A little girl may be frightened and confused by the death of a relative who went to the hospital and did not come back. This is especially true if she was not permitted to attend the funeral, her parents avoided talking about the dead person, and she had no clear, concrete picture of what actually happened. She may feel that, if a person suddenly dies and disappears into nowhere, this can happen to anyone, especially to her or her parents. Her fantasy may create all sorts of fears and anxieties: fear of being abandoned by her parents for misbehavior, fear that her parents will suddenly die and disappear, fear that accidents and sickness will strike her and her parents. Such anxieties can grow into widespread phobias of all kinds and cause the child to withdraw from many normal activities. She may become emotionally disturbed, be unable to concentrate on her schoolwork, or insist on staying home to see that nothing happens to her or her parents.

How does attendance or nonattendance at a funeral influence

children's reactions to death? Denying children the right to attend a funeral tends to reflect the anxieties and concerns of the adult rather than the children's actual ability to cope with the situation. By attending the funeral the reality of the situation will be reinforced in the children's mind and prevent them from developing unrealistic ideas or fears about the death of a loved one. Parents and relatives should not be distressed that children attending a funeral will be exposed to crying and grieving. It is at times like these that children learn that having and expressing such feelings are normal. The facts of life are that adults do cry.

Schowalter makes some interesting points on the question of children and funerals. Funerals, according to Schowalter, are an accepted means of group mourning. They allow the bereaved an opportunity to be supported while expressing their grief. The community acknowledgment of the death provided by the funeral also acts to prevent excessive denial. The important question, then, is at what age or stage of development can participation in a funeral be supportive of children's capacity to recognize, accept, and work through the death of a close person?

Prior to the second half of their first year, infants are not able to see themselves separate from their surroundings. Funerals will have no direct meaning at this age. This is not to say that the death of a parent or sibling has no emotional impact on infants. The impact, however, is indirect and comes through the mourning survivors' inability to provide infants with their usual care.

Until children can grasp intellectually the meaning of a funeral, the event is likely to be an additional emotional burden for them to bear. It would be wrong to base one's decision about funeral attendance solely on developmental considerations. Death perceptions precede death conceptions, and the attitudes of important figures in children's lives may have a greater impact on their response to death than will their intellectual understanding. The less able children are to grasp intellectually the meaning of death, the more dependent they are on the emotional climate provided, and the more likely they are to misinterpret it. For this reason Schowalter feels that it is unusual for children under the age of six or seven years to experience funerals as a useful psychological event.[48]

The funeral should be explained in terms that describe how the family views it. The decision to go or not should be the adults', but around the age of six to eight, children should be asked if they wish to attend the funeral. If the child does not wish to go, that decision should be respected. Children who wish to go but are not allowed sometimes exaggerate the mystery of the funeral. Whether children go to the funeral or stay home, they should be accompanied by someone who is not so involved in the death and can give them undivided attention.

How children will react if they do attend the funeral will be predicted by their past experiences as well as their present support. Children who have been active in arranging funerals for pets or discovered dead animals often seem better able to experience their passive roles at the real thing. If the deceased is a distant friend or relative, children are usually better able to handle the funeral than if the death is of a parent, sibling, or someone else to whom they are very close. How often they have attended church or temple and how comfortable they are with the services are also important considerations.

The particular circumstances of the death of a loved one is an additional factor that influences children's reactions to the death. Variables such as quickness or slowness, painfulness or painlessness, will have their effect. If the death took place under honorable or dishonorable circumstances, accidentally or from old age, in the child's presence or absence, the result and reaction will be different in each case.

Death of parents caused by such unexpected disasters as tornadoes, floods, or earthquakes have a shocking effect on children. When the death of a parent is caused by a sudden accident, the shock can be overwhelming. If a member of the family, a son perhaps, indirectly caused the accident, he may never forgive himself. The family may either blame him outright, or may try to protect him from his feelings of guilt and transfer the blame elsewhere—on

God or fate, for example. But when the death is a suicide, the entire family may be filled with guilt and shame. If the parent dies of a lingering fatal illlness, the children who have been prepared for it may gradually learn to accept their bereavement.

Children take their cue on how to react to the death of a parent by observing how their relatives conduct themselves, and by being told what to do. They must feel that they are part of the family and participate in all the customs and ceremonies that are part of dealing with death.

The children's relation to the person who died has a definite influence on their reaction. Different effects and reactions can be observed in the case of the loss of a mother, father, or sibling. The death of either parent uproots the entire family and deprives it of emotional and financial support. Children may feel lost without the loved parent to turn to for guidance and affection. The death of either parent influences the role they must play in the family and society.

Children need their parents at all ages, but their age and the degree of their dependence make a difference in how much the loss affects their lives. Younger children feel deprived when they see their peers participating in activities that include fathers, such as Boy Scouts. They are definitely affected by the loss, and they envy other children who have a father.

The teenage son who is faced with his father's death has to be helped to find his rightful role in the surviving family. His mother wants him to be the "man of the house" and his siblings expect him to take their father's place at a time when he himself needs a father as a guide. Opportunities for education, social and recreational experiences that are a part of youth and growing towards maturity— all may be greatly altered by the father's death. The son becomes angry and depressed that joy and freedom have gone out of his life and left sadness and sorrow. He is filled with confusion, resentment, and guilt.

The surviving family needs to help every member share in the responsibilities that arise at the death of a father; no child should be expected to give up his or her own right of self-fulfillment.

The death of the mother in a family is very traumatic to her children. Their age is important in the way their mothers' death affects their future development. Krinsky indicates that children who have been deprived of mothering and who have formed no personal human bonds during the first two years show permanent impairment of the capacity to make human attachments in later childhood. Their future development will be influenced by the type of mothering they receive from the substitute. If the substitute mother gives them loving care that is supported by the father, the loss of the children's mother will be lessened as they develop feelings of trust and security in the mother substitute.

In some adults, Krinsky notes, the disturbance caused by loss in childhood is hidden but is damaging to their lives. They are unable to feel close to anyone. Their relationships are shallow and meaningless. A portion of affective life is cut off because they do not want to become involved and be hurt by another loss.[49]

In summarizing the nature of children's reactions to a parent's death, Miller states that a nearly unanimous position among researchers has been found to exist. The position is based on the conclusion that children, in comparison to adults, do not pass through a mourning that includes the gradual and painful emotional detachment from the person who has died.

Miller further indicates that only two major contributors to the childhood parent-loss area hold that mourning is found in children. Even these two, Kliman and Furman, claim to observe mourning in children only under exceptional circumstances, which involve active clinical efforts to facilitate the mourning process and intensive counseling of significant adults in the children's lives. These writers stress promoting the expression of sad effect and do not claim that the process of internal emotional decathexis actually occurs in children. Bowlby, who previously held the view that the reaction to separation from the mother was a genuine mourning process, has modified this view to conform to the position that reaction to parental death in childhood is not mourning but rather a complex series of defensive responses aimed at denying the reality of the event.

Children's reactions to the death of a sibling are different than to the death of a parent. Guilt and fear are the two most common reactions observed. Some sibling rivalry is part of every family, and children may experience the loss of a sibling as the result of their feelings of envy, or their anger at the intruding child. This then arouses guilt and anxiety about being punished for having caused the death. The parents can help children cope with the loss of a sibling by realistically indicating what happened to the deceased child; being aware that the children are going to form some explanation of why the death occurred and helping with the feelings associated with this; and reassuring the children that their feelings were not the cause of the death.

Children's everyday encounters with life and death can also influence their responses and attitudes toward death. Zeligs sees a difference between rural and urban children's experiences with death and points out the effect this difference in exposure may have on children's reactions to death. Rural children have more opportunities than urban children to witness the birth and death of living things so that the meaning of death becomes more a reality to them. Country children are close to nature. All around them they see living and growing things. They watch the sprouting seed and the growth of flowers and fruit. They see the birth of calves and other animals. Just as they experience life through close contacts, they are also exposed to death. They learn to accept death as a reality and part of life.

City children, on the other hand, are separated from nature by the walls of houses and cement. Although schools sometimes have animals in the classroom, it is not enough. When death occurs, city children may be surprised and shocked because they are far from nature and its constant cycle of life and death.[50]

In conclusion, it may be said that children's reactions to death are influenced by numerous factors. Of all the factors discussed, I tend to agree with Schowalter and others who feel that probably the most important influence on how young children act around the time of a death is the response of their parents and other adults around them. When a sibling dies, children temporarily lose their parents too, in the psychological and emotional sense, since the parents may be so overcome by their own loss that they have little emotional support to give the surviving children.

Unable to understand the permanence of death, young children may consider adults' behavior excessive. On the other hand, children's developmental inability to mourn in a manner similar to adults often disturbs relatives and friends. They may find the children's frequent hyperactivity, concern for concrete matters such as food, and lack of sadness as irritating signs of insensitivity. Since guilt is one of children's typical reactions to death, when they are scolded for not acting in a way they are not able to, their confusion and guilt will only be increased.

Children's "mourning" for the death of a significant person in their lives requires a good deal of understanding patience. Like adults, children have a need to work through their grief and anxieties. They should share their feelings, both positive and negative, about the deceased with the family. Their recollections of the dead person should be encouraged, as should participation in discussions with the family about the future.

Normal, emotionally healthy children can successfully cope with the experience of losing a sibling or parent through death. With patience and consideration, children can be aided in dealing with such loss. Children need special consideration in many areas. They need an opportunity to talk about their loss; they must be helped to realize that life around them continues, and they must contribute to it in spite of their loss. Their life style may be changed, but with the proper help they can adapt to the changes. The suffering that children undergo with the death of a family member can be a growth experience if handled properly by the adults around them.

4

Death and the Child: The Psychological Aspects

> *". . . healthy children will not fear life
> if their elders have integrity enough
> not to fear death."*
> —Erik H. Erikson,
> *Childhood and Society*

In the past, death was a very important part of family life. Loved ones died at home, where adults and children both shared in the death experience. Death has changed from being an expected and accepted part of a child's life to a somewhat rare occurrence. Children today usually graduate from high school without ever experiencing the death of a loved one.[51]

Death has become an other-related event rather than a self-related event, because neither children nor their parents are in immediate danger of dying.[52] In fact, only about one in twenty children suffer the loss of a parent, through death, by the time they are eighteen years old.[53]

A 1957 study of male children from five to sixteen years old, by Alexander and Adlerstein, found that more emotion was aroused by words associated with death than by other words. Nine- to twelve-year-olds were aroused less emotionally than the younger and older groups. Alexander and Adlerstein concluded that death affected this group of children less because they are in a tranquil stage of development.

Children, by seeing dead animals and watching television, become aware of death at a very early age and may even inquire about it. When adults avoid talking about the subject, children interpret this to mean the subject is to be avoided. Children come to the conclusion that death must be bad if their parents won't discuss it with them. In effect, adults cause children more grief by not talking to them about death. This causes children not to tell adults how they feel about death.

A delicate balance must be found that will allow children to express their ideas about death. This is necessary because a child might not be able to psychologically handle the subject of death. In trying to find this balance between avoidance and confrontation, adults have to:

1. try to be sensitive to [children's] desire to communicate when they're ready;
2. try not to put up barriers that may inhibit [children's] attempts to communicate;
3. offer children honest explanations when we are obviously upset;
4. listen to and accept the child's feelings;
5. answer the child's questions, instead of putting them off by telling them they're too young.[54]

The person who is keenly alive, and whose capacity to experience feeling is highly developed, can best cope with death, though the loss will be felt deeply.

Children need to express, in some manner, the intense emotions they feel about death, rather than letting them accumulate and explode at a later time.

According to Sylvia Anthony, a pioneer in the study of children and death, children and uneducated adults base their reasoning abilities on what they see. Some of the logical conclusions derived from these observations are:

1. The body and soul are two separate entities. This reasoning is based, for example, on the observation that, while asleep, they

see and feel things that are not dependent on body participation.

2. Time is not constant. It is also observed to be progressive and never digresses for anyone.

3. All living things observed by a child die. For example, flowers and animals eventually die.[55]

Another factor influencing children in the formulation of their ideas is that the language they are learning to use has many strange references to death. The car will not start because the battery is *dead*. In a dart game, while *killing* time, someone throws one *dead* center. An exasperated father yells to *kill* the light after he has come home *dead* tired, because he has spent all day with *deadbeats* who are trying to make a *killing* in the market. On the other hand, adults try to avoid the use of the words *dead* or *die* when death itself is actually the subject. So we put pets *to sleep*, and people *pass on* or are lost or expire "when we really mean they're dead."[56]

When children reach the age of ten, they usually view death much as adults do. They also may start to question death rituals and customs. An eleven-year-old said, "My grandfather was all dressed up with makeup on and shoes. We had to buy a new suit, and it's going to rot away. I don't know why they did that."[57] A ten-year-old said, "You're at rest, and nobody can bother you. In a way, it's good and not bad. I imagine my grandpa in heaven, sitting in a chair with a big cigar in his mouth and no bills to pay."[58]

According to researchers, the major influences on how children perceive death are their developmental stage and their life experience. From the age of ten through adolescence, children begin to realize that death is a one-way process that is inevitable. Some children try to develop philosophical views of life and death, while others react to their fears by taking daring chances with their lives.

The rate at which children experience life, express and handle feelings, depends on the individual. Some children may not be affected by the death of a grandparent, but will react deeply to the death of a pet.

Children often feel guilty about the death of a close relative and sometimes think that they caused the death.

We must realize that anger is an important part of grief reactions. Therefore, children should not be scolded for expressing feelings of anger.

Grief reactions in children take on many forms, and it is extremely important for a mourning child to exhibit some type of grief reaction.

Some possible reactions to death are:

1. SHOCK

   Many people experience shock when told that a loved one has died. Their mind appears to be elsewhere, as they lose touch with reality.[59]

2. SOMATIC SYMPTOMS

   It has been found that when people experience acute grief they often exhibit a change in body symptoms. Some of the common symptoms of bereavement are shallowness of breath, fatigue, insomnia, and loss of appetite.

   Some common responses of children experiencing bodily distress are: "I have a tightness in my throat!" "My stomach hurts!" "I can't sleep!"

3. DENIAL

   The first step in the mourning process is testing and accepting the reality of the loss. Children's denial of death is a result of their unwillingness to accept its finality. Some typical denial responses are: "I don't believe it." "It didn't happen." "It's just a dream." "He can't die; he's my brother!"

4. ANGER AND GUILT

   Grieving children often have reactions of anger. They might aim their hostility at innocent bystanders because they haven't experienced the same loss. Many children have feelings of guilt because they think they caused the death of a loved one.[60]

Children often blame doctors and nurses for not using technology to its utmost to save their loved ones. Hostile feelings are even directed at the deceased person for causing so much grief and loneliness.

5.EMBARRASSMENT

Many children experience embarrassment when a parent or sibling dies. They know that they did not cause the death of their mother or father or sibling, but they still feel uncomfortable and are humiliated when the topic comes up.

6.DEPRESSION

Depression is experienced by most children who are grieving. They often feel hopeless and emotionally drained.[61]

7.FEAR

Children who have experienced death often fear that death will strike again. Some of the following questions concerning fear are asked by children who have lost a parent: "Who will take care of me now?" "Daddy used to bring home money for food and toys." If a sibling dies the child may anxiously wonder, "Will I die too?"

8.CURIOSITY

Children are naturally curious about death and they will openly show their curiosity until, through adult influence, they learn that the subject is considered taboo.

9.SADNESS

It is common for children to feel sad after a death of a loved one. When this happens, they are unhappy for a while, but they quickly become happy again. The intensity of grief may be too much for the child to bear for a prolonged period.

10. REPLACEMENT

Grieving children might try to substitute the love of others for that of the deceased parent or sibling. They may ask for reassurance from the surviving parent or substitute another child for the lost sibling.

11. ASSUMPTION OF MANNERISMS OF DECEASED

Children often emulate the deceased parent. For example, a boy might try to assume his deceased father's mannerisms by talking and walking like him. The child may adopt characteristics of the dead sibling, such as taste in clothes or hobbies.

The next type of grief reactions are those caused by suicide. When a suicide occurs, it is important that children be reassured about their safety because violent deaths may rouse misconceptions that children may have about their immediate environment.

When a suicide occurs, the mourning process is often interrupted, because the family tries to hide the cause of death from the public.

Since children may not understand the circumstances surrounding suicide, they may try to experiment with suicidal behaviors. For example, they may ask, "What would happen if I jumped off the roof or lit the stove myself?"

Case histories reveal that children whose parents have committed suicide are more apt to exhibit suicidal tendencies than other children. If a parent or sibling commits suicide, it might be wise for the surviving family to seek counseling together. Seeing suicide as a solution to life's stresses can be avoided.

Because of the social stigma associated with suicide, families try to hide their mourning and feelings about the death. They try to act as if the person who committed suicide never existed. This type of behavior may have long-lasting effects on the child.

If a child is made to feel that death is shameful, the mourning process may be delayed.

The death of a parent, brother, or sister are the hardest for a child to cope with. As a result, emotional and mental problems may occur.

There is a thin line between normal psychological mourning reactions and unnatural mourning reactions. Unnatural reactions might be a continued denial of the death even months after the event, apathy, prolonged anxiety and bodily distress, persistent hostility to the deceased or others, and excessive idealization.

There is no clear-cut way of determining when a child may need outside help. Professional help should be sought if the following symptoms occur: regressive changes in bowel and bladder control, persistent sleep problems, excessive aggression, hyperactivity, prolonged loss of ability to concentrate, and wild alternations in emotion or expression of thought, which seem markedly different than the child's previous behavior.

Caution should be taken if mourning never occurs in a child. Some of the effects that may occur as a result of delayed or unexpressed grief are:

1. problems in school
2. juvenile delinquency
3. sullen withdrawal
4. promiscuity
5. unwillingness to make friends[62]

Coping with the inevitability of death, and expressing our feelings and reactions when someone we love dies, helps us to survive.

The best rule for adults to follow is to be honest when talking to children about death. The use of euphemisms should be avoided when explaining death. For example, telling children that a dead person has gone to sleep might cause them to fear going to sleep. Or children who are told that God took someone in death might become angry or fearful of God.

Death is an integral part of life, and a healthy attitude toward it can only enhance life. Childhood experiences are often the foundation for how adults view life. Early positive death education is essential for children.

5

The Child and Family: Facing a Terminal Illness

Cancer is the second most common cause of death in the United States. Approximately 365,000 Americans die annually from cancer, with an incidence rise of about 2 percent per year. Over 40 million persons are being treated for cancer, and more than one person dies from cancer every two minutes. Forty years ago, fewer than 20 percent of Americans diagnosed with cancer survived. Today 33 percent survive. Cancer affects every age group from birth to senescence, both sexes, and every part of the body. Two thousand children under the age of fifteen die of cancer each year.

Not only is cancer a threat to life, but its cost in money, loss of production, disrupted lives, and human suffering is incalculable. No estimates can be made of loss of potential leadership and talent when a child dies of cancer. Expenses such as loss of income, housekeeping services, and increased household budgets cannot be accurately estimated. Cancer care costs are exhorbitant in hospital bills, outpatient therapy and followup, and services of doctors and nurses.[63]

Cancer is now the number-one cause of death from *disease* in children between one and fifteen years of age. Its incidence is approximately ten per one hundred thousand children annually. Acute leukemia is the most common malignancy in children, with twenty-five hundred new cases reported in children every year. It occurs in nearly four per hundred thousand children. Since leukemia is marked by exacerbations and remissions of physical illness, the dying trajectory may extend three to five years.[64] The diagnosis of leukemia in a child disrupts family life. Both child and family need long-term support—social, physical, emotional, psychological, and spiritual.

Psychological Impact of Life-Threatening Disease

Living with a life-threatening disease requires psychological adjustments by the patients and their family. These adjustments take place in stages and usually begin with the announcement of the diagnosis.

CRISIS OF DISCOVERY

For parents, the crisis of discovery begins when they are told the diagnosis of the fatal illness. No single event, with the exception of the child's death itself, has a greater impact on the life of a family. Many parents state that they had suspected that their child had a fatal disease before actually being told the diagnosis by the physician. Typically, parents respond by being stunned, shocked, or disbelieving when hearing a definitive diagnosis. Most parents initially feel guilt and self-blame for not having paid more attention to the early nonspecific manifestations of the disease. Many wonder if the child would have had a better chance of responding to therapy if the diagnosis had been made earlier. This self-blame is characteristically a transient phenomenon. More often, parents blame themselves for not having been more appreciative of the child before his or her illness. This attitude frequently leads to overindulgence and overprotection of the fatally ill child, with no limits put on the child's behavior. Friedman interprets the shock as an extreme degree of isolation of affect, a mechanism by which the apparent intellectual recognition of a painful event is not associated with a concomitant intolerable emotional response. He reported this lack of affective experience continued to be a conspicuous defense and enabled parents to talk realistically about their child's condition and prognosis with relatively little evidence of emotional involvement.[65]

Typically, the dying child's grandparents tend to be less accepting of the diagnosis than the parents. More distant relatives and friends challenge the reality of the diagnosis even more frequently. Parents generally perceive most of these statements and suggestions as attempts to cheer them up and give them hope. Yet, parents often find themselves in the uncomfortable position of having to "defend" their child's diagnosis and prognosis. Sometimes the parents reported feeling that other people thought they were condemning their own child. Thus, these parents were not allowed to express any feelings of hopelessness, yet paradoxically they were expected to appear grief-stricken.

The reactions of children at the time of diagnosis depends upon a number of factors, including their age, what they are told about what is happening to them, and whether they are hospitalized. If their diagnosis is made during an acute episode of the disease, they may display little psychological response or open expression of emotion because their energies are being used in combating the disease process.

Richmond reported that, in the children he observed, there was rarely manifested overt concern about death. Richmond interprets this as an attempt at psychological repression of anxiety concerning death. In general, his children seemed to have reacted with an air of passive acceptance and resignation. Associated with this often seemed to be an atmosphere of melancholia.[66]

Although children may not understand the diagnosis, the prognosis, or the therapy, they are adept at reading messages and picking up clues and signals from those around them. Very young children perceive what is happening on a feeling level. Their parents are suddenly protective to the point of smothering them. Regression, temper tantrums, or various other forms of misbehavior may suddenly be allowed. Children as young as eight months old have been observed reacting to their parents' emotional reaction to bad news.[67]

The home life of the family generally centers on the terminally ill child. Both parents and siblings sacrifice time, money, and energy for the ill child. Parents admitted that the other children in the family were neglected during the illness. Social events are not enjoyed by the family, and parents feel guilty about being happy.

DYING TRAJECTORY

Discovery of a fatal disease marks the beginning of the dying trajectory. With diseases such as leukemia, the dying trajectory may extend three to five years, though some survive for even longer periods. Both child and family have to live with the ambiguities of an uncertain future. The adaptational tasks of these families require the parents to maintain an investment in the welfare and the future of the ill child, while at the same time preparing for death through anticipatory grieving. Parents need to maintain a sense of mastery, while at the same time knowing the terminal nature of the child's illness. The child needs to integrate the losses and changes produced by the illness, while still fulfilling whatever personal potential for life exists.

Stages of Psychological Adjustment

The process of learning to live with a life-threatening illness takes place in stages. All involved—family members, the child, and health care members—go through a series of stages in which they assimilate the changes in the child's status into their own concept of reality. The first stage is shock and disbelief, during which denial is a commonly observed pattern of behavior. Anger or guilt and a gradual awareness of the change in the child's condition may occur next. One must reorganize relationships with other people, and one may attempt to strike a bargain with God to have death postponed. Resolution of the loss through active grieving must occur. There should also be reorganization of identity incorporating the loss of the loved one.

These stages do not necessarily take place in a certain order or in an easy manner. People generally have to repeat the stages each time the child goes through a serious episode of physical regression and/or hospitalization.

People vary in their capacity to experience and openly display their anger, frustation, guilt, sadness, and grief. Persons who have been taught to openly express these emotions will usually move through the stages of psychological adaptation more easily than those who think of overt expression as a sign of weakness or loss of control.

AWARENESS OF DEATH

A problem of great concern for parents of a child with a fatal ill-ness is how much the child knows, or should know, about the diag-nosis and prognosis. According to Glaser and Strauss, the behavior of dying persons and their interaction with others is influenced by the "awareness context" in which it takes place. Glaser and Strauss define an awareness context as "what each interacting person knows of the patient's defined status, along with his recognition of the other's awareness of his own definition . . . it is the context with-in which these people interact while taking cognizance of it . . . it may change over time." They define the types of awareness contexts as: closed awareness, suspected awareness, mutual-pretense aware-ness, and open awareness. In the closed-awareness context, patients do not recognize their impending death, although everyone else does. The suspected-awareness context occurs when patients sus-pect what others know and attempt to confirm or negate their sus-picions. In the mutual-pretense context, everyone defines the pa-tient as dying, but each pretends that the others have not done so. In the open-awareness context, the patient and all of the others are aware that death is imminent and express it openly.[68]

Glaser and Strauss stress that the impact of each type of aware-ness context influences the interaction between patient, family, and staff. Actions and conversations are guided by who knows what and with what degree of certainty. They argue that action, talk, and accompanying clues cause certain awareness contexts to develop in-to other contexts. This occurs when one of the persons in the inter-action violates the rules necessary for maintaining that particular context. A new context then develops.

MUTUAL-PRETENSE CONTEXT

Bluebond-Langner argues that, in the case of leukemic children, once they become aware of their prognosis, they practice mutual pretense until death in spite of violation of the rules. Breaches in the rules of mutual pretense do not lead to open awareness as they do with the terminally ill adults Glaser and Strauss studied.[69]

Bluebond-Langner argues that conditions necessary for the development of mutual pretense are present from the moment the children enter the hospital, even before the diagnosis is made. The hospital staff is structured to keep information from the patients, guard against leaks, and cover up if leaks do occur. Parents help to set up the mutual-pretense context when children start to ask probing questions about their illness. Parents volunteer very little information and explain as little as possible. Dangerous topics, such as holidays, future plans, the child's appearance, and the drugs being used, are avoided. Topics of conversation include the daily routine, ward activities, zoos, books, and other nonthreatening items. Bluebond-Langner postulates that the children take this as a signal that their parents are unwilling to talk about their condition. When children realize they are dying and that people are no more willing to talk about their condition than they had ever been, the children start to practice mutual pretense. Only two of the forty children in this study practice open awareness.

Bluebond-Langner argues that leukemic children's awareness and communications concerning death and dying are different from adults'. She bases her assumptions upon a modern perspective of childhood socialization and social order. She argues that four factors should be studied in the socialization of children: "acquisition of information about the world, self, and others; experience with others and with oneself in that world; changes in self concept; and the order to which one is being socialized."[70]

Bluebond-Langner reports that leukemic children acquire detailed information about the world, self, and others from a variety of sources. She reports that the children know the institution and the disease as well as any lay adult. Children rapidly acquire knowledge of hospital order and structure. They know covert and overt functions of the various rooms, written and unwritten rules, hospital regulations and procedures. They demonstrate knowledge of the social organization and tasks of hospital personnel. The primary source of their information appears to be peers—other leukemic children. They also obtain information from hospitalized nonleukemic children, overheard conversations, and direct observation of other children in the oncology clinic.

Bluebond-Langner proposed that leukemic children acquire factual information about their disease in five stages. She represents these stages as:

dx	1	2	3	4	5
	"it" is a serious disease	names of drugs and side effects	purposes of treatments and procedures	disease as a series of relapses and remissions (– death)	disease as a series of relapses and remissions (+ death)

Bluebond-Langner states that each stage is marked by the acquisition of disease-related information. Particular experiences are critical to passage through these stages and to the socialization process. Experiences such as nosebleeds or bone pain enable the children to gather significant information. At any sign of illness, the children are taken to the clinic, where they can meet with their peers and discuss what is happening to them. The experience also enables them to assimilate this information by relating what they see and hear to their own experience. They see children at the clinic who are pale, frail, edematous, and bald. The children do not ask about things that are not happening to them.

Bluebond-Langner postulates that the relationship of experience in the socialization process explains why a child could remain at a given stage without passing to the next for unusual lengths of time. She finds age and intellectual ability unrelated to the speed or completeness with which children pass through the stages. Some three- and four-year-old children of average intelligence know more about their prognosis than some very intelligent nine-year-olds who are still in their first remission, have had fewer clinic visits, and thus less experience.

Bluebond-Langner reports that as the children pass through the five stages of acquisition of information, they also pass through five different stages of self-concept. These different self-concepts are represented as:

dx	1	2	3	4	5
well	seriously ill	seriously ill and will get better	always ill and will get better	always ill and will never get better	dying (terminally ill)

Bluebond-Langner postulates that the children's view of themselves is the result of the various kinds of information that they have acquired in interactions with others, as well as through personal experiences.

Bluebond-Langner argues that it is clear that terminally ill children know they are dying before death becomes imminent. She argues that leukemic children, their parents, and staff engage in mutual pretense because it enables each of them to fulfill the roles and responsibilities necessary for maintaining membership in the society. This gives credence to the illusion of their normalcy and allows others to do what is expected of them. The children demonstrate awareness of their social obligations and responsibilities and their competence in social matters.

Mutual pretense helps parents prepare for the final separation by pacing it out and allowing them to rehearse the separation in an acceptable manner. The children's use of distancing strategies give parents an excuse to leave without feeling they are deserting the child. Parents feel that protecting children means shielding them from knowledge of the disease, diagnosis, and prognosis. Parents who assume this context and let their children know it by nonverbal cues are also not put in the position of having to answer difficult questions.

Mutual pretense protects the family members temporarily against too much grief and the staff members against too immediate a scene. The dying person may be denied a closer relationship with family members and staff, which sometimes occurs with open acceptance.

Open Awareness

Advocates of the open-awareness approach argue that children with a fatal illness and their siblings need an enviroment in which they can ask questions and can know what is happening. Those parents give the children information about their illness and their future.

An awareness of impending death gives patients an opportunity to close their lives in the manner they wish. Open awareness has disadvantages too. Other people may not approve of the patients' way of managing their death and may attempt to change their ideas.

Bluebond-Langner's study revealed only two children who were able to develop an open awareness context. She stresses that it is the child, not the adult, who develops the open-awareness context. The shift to open awareness does not result from a breakdown in the mutual-pretense context. When open awareness is achieved it is not necessarily final or complete in every area. There are lapses back to mutual pretense when the child achieves a remission.

She finds that parents of these children are different from those who practice mutual pretense. These parents seem to derive most of their identity and sense of self-worth from sources other than the parental role. These parents are also more unconventional in their behavior and appear less concerned about society's judgment of their beliefs.

These parents also experience additional problems. They are sometimes ostracized by their peers and staff for not protecting their child from the facts. Staff members appear not to be as helpful to these parents. Parents are also faced with more concrete problems of how to treat and what to say to the child. Yet, these parents say that being honest with their child has helped them to cope with the prognosis. Honesty also has helped to bring them closer together.

Conclusions

Bluebond-Langner reports that children practicing mutual pretense and open awareness behaved in the same manner. Both sets of
children are preoccupied with death and disease imagery in their
play, art, and conversation. They do not discuss going home and future plans, and they continue to practice distancing strategies.[71]

Bluebond-Langner argues that the question is not "Should I tell
the child that he or she is dying?" but "Should I acknowledge the
prognosis to the child?" She recommends that the needs of the
child, family, and staff be taken into consideration. She recommends allowing the child to maintain open awareness with those
who can handle it and, at the same time, mutual pretense with
those who cannot. She suggests telling children only what they
want to know, what they are asking about, and on their own level.
The issue is not whether to tell children that they are dying, but
how to tell them in a way that respects them and their needs.

The Terminal State

The terminal state is divided into three stages: the terminal phase,
the terminal period, and the terminal event.

The Terminal Phase

The terminal phase may last weeks or months. The child may
have frequent relapses, difficult remissions, and numerous complications. This phase marks a renewal of bargaining—for experimental procedures and finally for enough medication to relieve the
child's pain.

Those involved with the dying child are often angry at this time.
Parents may become angry if others talk about their child's future
when it is so obvious that the child has none.

Children at this stage often lose interest in the outside world.
They may become more depressed with each discharge from the
hospital because they have accepted the painful reality that they can
no longer participate in and enjoy the activities of family and friends.
Older children know they will never get well and may wish that

death would come. Rarely do older children resist to the end. Older children are usually resigned to their death before their family is and they often feel guilty. Many children thank their parents for all they have done for them or ask forgiveness for the problems their illness has caused.

The Terminal Period

During the terminal period the inevitability of death is recognized and affirmed. This stage may be more readily reached when children are free from pain and appear at peace with themselves. Sometimes when pain is great, acceptance or resignation becomes easier. Parents may say that they accept the inevitability of the child's death, but they do not always believe it. True acceptance means realizing that there is no hope for survival.

When death is near, the family may have to make a decision about whether the child will die at home. Decisions must also be made about transplants and an autopsy.

Children in the terminal period of their illness often, quite deliberately, will stop talking about discharge, returning to school, or any future plans. They may become depressed or withdrawn. Some preschoolers with a perfect understanding of tenses have been noted to talk about their aspirations in the past tense.

Chinn reports that in some instances where parents and children have experienced a very supportive and close relationship up to this point, they may mutually "recognize" the termination of further energy resources. Such children may begin to help their parents to stay away or to transfer their interest to other people and things. The children may find it too painful to watch their parents mourn. They may bid their parents goodbye too soon and may be left alone to die.[72]

The Terminal Event

The terminal event includes the hours preceding death itself. A child may rally before death and achieve a surprising alertness. Some parents regard this as a last treasured gift, others as a painful experience since they know so little time is left and there is so much to talk about.

Friedman reports that the child's death is generally taken calmly, but with the appropriate expressions of effect. Outbursts of uncontrollable grief or open expressions of self-blame are the exception. Usually there is some indication of relief that the child is no longer suffering. Friedman suggests that, therefore, the death of the child does not appear to be a severe superimposed stressful situation but, rather, an anticipated loss at the end of a long sequence of events.[73]

Bereavement

Following the death of a loved one, three phases of grief occur.

PHASE 1. SHOCK AND DISBELIEF

During this phase the bereaved are intensely preoccupied with the image of the deceased. Mourners commonly experience somatic distress that occurs in waves lasting twenty to sixty minutes. They experience an empty feeling in the abdomen, lack of muscular power, a feeling of tightness in the throat, a need for sighing, and choking with shortness of breath. The bereaved are also strongly preoccupied with feelings of guilt. They magnify incidences with the dead one in which they may have been negligent.

PHASE 2. DEVELOPING AWARENESS

The bereaved experience a disorganization of personality in this phase. They feel a persistent and insatiable yearning for the dead person. This phase is characterized by pain, despair, weeping, and a feeling of helplessness.

PHASE 3. RESOLVING THE LOSS

The bereaved recognize and accept the loss of the dead person and begin to form new relationships with other persons.

Mourning or grieving is successfully completed when the bereaved can remember completely and realistically the pleasures and disappointments of the lost relationship.

Reintegration of the Family

Anglim reports that reintegration of the family after the child's death is related to several factors. These factors include attitudes developed before death and activities engaged in prior to death.

Families that remained actively involved in the child's care and the decision-making process seemed more able to resolve their grief after the child's death. The maintenance of their role as parents during the dying trajectory seemed to strengthen their view of themselves as parents and individuals. Fulfilling their role expectations seemed to also strengthen the appreciation of husband and wife for one another.

After the child's death, the family faces a new identity and members of the families are faced with new roles. They are no longer a family with a terminally ill child. There is a dramatic difference in the mobility and flexibility of the family without such a child.

Families find few friends or relatives willing to talk about the dead child. Peer-support groups that have been established before the death of the child seem to help. Groups started after the death appear to some families as "therapy" and are rejected unless desperately needed.[74]

Most families experience what would be considered a normal grieving process, but these are tempered by the relief of knowing that the child is no longer suffering.

Sibling reaction to the death must be considered in reference to their age and concept of death, as explained in the previous sections. Religious beliefs sometimes make it easier to explain the death to a sibling. Most remaining siblings are overprotected by their parents. Many parents have a tendency to check siblings for the disease symptoms of the dead child.

Conclusion

Terminally ill children and their families need long-term support—physically, socially, psychologically, and spiritually. More home care and hospice programs need to become available and accessible to dying children and their families soon.

6

Care for the Dying Child

Terminal care is becoming an increasingly accepted practice in the medical community. As part of the terminal care program, the patient's house is often chosen as the place for continued care, as well as the site for death of the patient. Even though this practice has been increasingly instituted with older dying patients, it very rarely has been considered an option for the terminally ill child. It has been a commonly accepted belief that better care and greater control of pain and other symptoms associated with the illness are available in the hospital.

This belief, often felt by both the health care professionals and the family, fails to take into account the most important person, the child. Children's feelings often are overlooked, and decisions about their well-being are made by adults who "know best." In this chapter, the feelings and desires of terminally ill children will be examined in response to their care. Special emphasis will be directed in understanding the reaction to home care and its effect on dying children and their family, as well as the feasibility of its application.

What the Child Should Be Told

As has often been the case, the child is neglected when faced with a life-threatening illness. Much of the time and energy of the health care deliverer is spent helping the parents cope with the psychological upheaval of tending to a terminally ill child. Even though it is necessary to understand the problems of the parents, it is cruel to overlook the needs of the child.

In the past, it was believed that children could not understand the meaning of their illness, let alone be able to deal emotionally with its prospects if they were told. The results of further research have shown that children know the seriousness of their disease, and often the diagnosis, without being told directly. Surprisingly, sick children may be aware of their illness from as young an age as four. Since children do have such an accurate idea of the fate that approaches, the need to talk to them is even greater. The lack of discussion or acknowledgment to children as to the seriousness of their illness may lead to a feeling of isolation. Children may believe that others are not aware of what they are experiencing, or even worse, they may feel that their disease is "too awful" to talk about.

It has been shown that it is most beneficial to the children to make sure they know that their parents and physician can answer their questions and are willing to discuss the sickness when the need arises. So when first dealing with the child, it is important to establish a relationship that allows for questions, where it is understood that no barriers exist in discussing the topic of death. Children are capable of talking about death, and if they ask questions concerning their own death, this indicates that they really want to know.

There have been no established criteria as to how much to tell children, but it is believed that the best method is to let them lead the way. If they are allowed to be comfortable when asking questions, they will ask those questions that are most pertinent, and when satisfied with the information received, will generally feel more assured. It may take children weeks or even months to feel secure enough to ask those questions, but it is important that the opportunity always exists for their questions to be asked and that they are always made aware of this.[75]

When explaining the illness to the child, both the physician and parents should have a positive approach. The child reacts much more to how something is said than to what is said. Thus the child is more impressed by the implied, positive thinking conveyed by both the physician and parents. But both the physician and parents should beware of oversimplifying or relating the disease to a concept the child cannot fully comprehend. The best approach may be to draw the explanation as much as possible from the child's own experience. This allows for the least possible amount of distortion to be made by the child. To assure even further that the issue has not become more complicated by the explanations, it is a good idea to ask the child to explain back what he or she has been told. This allows one to correct any misconceptions the child may have before they can cause any further damage.

A point that needs to be considered by both physician and parents is that children should be told of their diagnosis and its implications even if they don't ask for the information. The reasoning behind this is that a child may be told by a playmate, which may cause later emotional problems and distrust toward the physician or parents. If the illness is made known by adults, the child will cope by denying the illness and will be able to withstand any shock when told accidentally by a friend.[76]

Home Care for Dying Children

From the inception of modern medical care, hospitals have been the setting for the treatment of children with cancer, including those who are terminally ill. The benefit of any continued hospital care is increasingly questioned once it is understood that there is no chance of the cancer becoming controlled. The trend today is toward alternative care: in the case of the terminally ill child, home care. More and more advantages are being found in relation to the quality of care the child receives and the benefits psychologically for the family.

In the recent past, hospitals have been the appropriate place for the ill to become cured and the terminally ill to die. There is no question that the hospital is where the best possible medical treatment can be received. No other institution has the power to prolong life or resuscitate the dying individual. People, however, increasingly are rejecting hospital care in favor of being allowed to die with dignity and in comfort. Probably one of the most ignored segments of the terminally ill population, insofar as having this desire fulfilled, is the youth of our society.

The hospital, though known for its power to care for the sick, has never been strong on giving the psychological support the patient needs. In the case of the dying child, the hospital seems to promote anxiety and discourage its relief. Terminally ill children react more strongly than would be expected to changes in their environment or family, such as fighting between the parents, changes in schools, moving, or separation. The hospital, then, would seem the last place to put the dying child for comfort and prolonged care. The most affected children, emotionally, are those of grade-school age who do not believe the hospital is for their own well-being. Instead, they feel they are being punished for the prospect of their own death. The parents are sending them away to die.

Once hospitalized, the pressures of separation and loneliness continue to mount for children. They may be subjected to either partial or total isolation, making it even more difficult for them to adapt to their situation.[77] This feeling is further reinforced when, in the hospital, continuous care by one doctor and regular visits rarely occur. Instead, care is provided by several physicians and there is no continuity. Children then have no one they can identify as their physician, and the patient-physician relationship, which can be so important, is never established.

Home care for the dying child avoids much of the emotional stress of the hospital. This was especially evident when, in a recent study, children dying of cancer "who were old enough to express an opinion, all preferred being at home to being in the hospital."[78] By being at home, children receive a variety of both psychological and social benefits. They are in a family environment where activities that have always been a part of their lives are taking place. The attention and discipline they are accustomed to is not withdrawn, as in the hospital, which can lead to confusion and unhappiness. At home, children receive the needed security and love that are intrinsic to the home environment.

In the hospital, the affection that children need is often not provided. Terminally ill children want more affection. However, they do not always make this need known. Often, instead of perceiving this greater need for affection, mothers of these children perceive quite the opposite. When this need goes unnoticed, children are lonely and frustrated.[79] This is less likely to occur in the home. There is no nurse who must see to the needs of a number of other patients, or a doctor who has other appointments to keep. At home, families can share the responsibilities in the care of dying children, as well as provide love and affection. So, just as the home is the natural place for children to be while living, it can also be a natural one for dying. Hence, children have their parents, they are in an environment of family surroundings, they can eat food they are used to, they are able to pursue normal activities as much as possible, and they can have the company of their brothers and sisters.

Home Care for the Family

There are differences in the roles and adjustments families of terminally ill children must make in opting for home care, rather than hospitalization. Children who are placed in the hospital not only become more anxious, but all the lives of the members of their families become more stressful. This is due to a number of factors. Probably foremost is the helpless feeling the family gets in trying to care for their child. Because of the structure and regimentation of hospital care, there is little that the family can do without the permission of someone on the hospital staff. Instead, it is the physicians and nurses who do the caring for the child and shoulder all responsibility for the child's well-being. The parents have no control over the situation, which makes them feel increasingly inadequate and helpless about their situation.[80]

The hospitalization of the dying child is not only stressful, but can be very inconvenient for the parents. Often the mother moves somewhere close to the hospital to be more of a comfort to the child, while the father works, maintains the home, and cares for any other siblings. One physician even suggests that food be made available that will tempt the child; the mother should bring in special dishes, or if the facilities are available, should cook for the child on the ward.[81] All of these suggestions or practices further increase the burden placed on the parents in trying to provide adequate care and attention for the child.

Another often overlooked consequence of hospitalization of the terminally ill child is its effect on the other siblings in the family. If the child dies in the hospital, the siblings may misinterpret the cause of death. Instead of seeing the hospital as a place where a sick brother or sister went to die, siblings may become confused about the cause of death. They may believe that the hospital, not the disease, killed their sibling.

Siblings of the dying child who has been hospitalized may have other psychological reactions. Often, they have feelings of guilt and fear that the same fate is awaiting them. Many siblings also feel rejected and unimportant, in response to the parents' preoccupation with the dying child.

In contrast, the members of the family are the primary care givers when home care for the dying child is instituted. The parents are able to take over as much of their child's care as they wish, with the health professionals providing the needed support.

In becoming the primary care givers, the family must make a few adjustments to their new role. The parents must fully understand that the child is dying and that, if the child is going to die at home, a sudden change in the child's condition is not necessarily a cause to go to the hospital. Thus, the parent must realize that the hospital is not esssential for providing pain control or other comforts that may be needed by a dying child, since pain can be controlled as well at home as in the hospital.

With these understandings, the family can now be receptive to the benefits that home care can provide for the dying child, as well as for themselves. The family is reunited to allow for a more "normal" daily living. When the dying child is at home, the parents do not disrupt their employment in order to spend time with the child. This usually is not the case when the child is hospitalized, though in some instances when the child is at home, the mother has the primary burden for the child's care. In these cases, the father continues to work full-time and the mother remains at home.

With the normal environment of the home reestablished, the desire of the parents to maintain an active role in their child's care, and to have constant access to their child, is fulfilled. In the environment of the home, the parent can treat the child "normally." They can live "day to day," "enjoy the child," "not give special privileges," and "not be overprotective"—actions and behaviors not encouraged when in the hospital environment.

With the child dying at home, the parents appear to derive much relief from stress. Since the child's death is inevitable, the parents feel more at ease since the home seems the natural place for their child to die. With the apparent decrease in possible anxiety, there appear to be a surprising number of beneficial results for the family. In fulfilling their child's wish to be at home, as well as their own, the parents may derive a considerable sense of satisfaction. This helps displace the feelings of guilt that frequently follow the death of the child. In support of this belief are the findings that parents who cared for their dying child at home seemed to return to "normal" sooner after the child's death. These parents went through the same grieving process as the parents of children who died in the hospital, but they were able to return to work and their other responsibilities sooner. These parents were able to dwell more on the positive aspects of their child's life, having been able to allay their feelings of guilt and avoid bitterness over the loss of their child. [82]

These same effects seem to be apparent in the siblings of the dead child. When the dying child is taken care of at home, the siblings may more easily establish the link between illness and death. This association does not usually occur when the sibling dies in the hospital, as discussed earlier. The siblings' lives also appear to return to normal sooner, with only short-term disruptions in schooling. Their needs for emotional support and reassurance that they are not going to die are given proper attention. [83]

The best example of the difference between families of the child who dies at home and the child who dies in the hospital can be found in two recently published studies. In approximately 50 percent of the families of children who died in the hospital, at least one member of the family reacted so strongly as to need psychiatric help. In contrast, almost no members of families of children who died at home required psychiatric help.[84]

Home Care Programs

Very few home care programs for the terminally ill child are reported in the literature. Dr. Ida Martinson, in 1972, initiated a home care program for children with cancer.

Martinson's project was developed as an alternative to hospitalization. She responded to: an increased awareness of patients' rights; an increased sensitivity to the total impact of the hospital on the child and family; and a concern for the sharply rising cost of the traditional health system.

Martinson's home care service was offered on the following basis: home care nurses were available twenty-four hours a day; home care nurses were available for visits whenever and wherever the family needed them; the option for the child's return to the hospital would remain open; the personal physician could be called at any time; and the home care nurse would try to help the family with any problem that arose.

Martinson primarily used two interventions: parental control and limiting uncertainty. In order to maintain parental control, Martinson did not give direct care to the child during the home visit. Procedures were carefully explained to the parents, and the parents then provided the care. This increased the parents' confidence in their ability to perform the basic skills needed to care for their child at home.[85]

To gain and maintain control, parents need effective and cognitive support. For effective support, parents were encouraged to call the nurse whenever they felt they needed advice or support. Cognitive support was given by preparing the parents for various complications that might occur.

Limiting uncertainty was achieved by giving information and explaining to the parents all the possibilities that might occur during this period, e.g., hemorrhaging. This helped to limit the uncertainty as to future events.

Pain was the most frequent reason for the family to seek immediate assistance from the health care nurse. Parents, reinforced by some health care professionals, reported a fear of addiction or tolerance. Home care was seen by some parents as a means of preventing or controlling the pain frequently associated with the hospital and medical procedures. All parents were able to initiate some unique comfort measures to reduce the child's perception of pain. These measures included: distraction, fantasy, sensory stimulation, and control of environmental variables that increased or decreased pain response.[86]

In the home care setting, the nurse acted as patient advocate in negotiating for alteration or procurement of drugs. The nurse supported the family, primarily the mother, in determining comfort measures that would minimize or alleviate pain.

Martinson reports that the home care program was cost effective. The majority of her patients died at home and the estimated home care cost was only $1,000. The average length of service to the family was forty-five days.[87]

Cost of Home Care

With all the benefits gained by both the child and family in home care, the question of monetary practicality should be raised. In home care, very little specialized equipment is needed. Those accessories that were required, such as bedpans, basins, and wheelchairs, had already been bought by the family during the course of their child's illness anyway. When comparing the difference in cost, the amount can be quite substantial. The cost of home care of the dying child averages about $25 per day. In contrast, hospital care costs range from $200 to $411 per day.[88]

Even with this vast difference in cost, in the final comparison home care may actually be more expensive than hospital care for the family. The way it is structured now, many insurance companies, which would normally cover the cost for hospitalization, will not reimburse the family for the expenses incurred when taking care of the child at home. So, although the overall savings are quite substantial, if home care is not part of their coverage, the family's costs could be increased.

The Roles of the Health Care Professionals

In the hope that care for the dying child will change and home care will be used successfully, the role of health care professionals must also change. Pivotal in its success is acceptance of the concept of terminal care by the health care staff. This may be especially hard for the pediatrician, who probably had very little training in dealing with the death of a patient. The overall rate of pediatric mortality has been decreasing, but there still has been an increasing number of pediatric cases involved with chronic illness, such as leukemia, cancer, and cystic fibrosis, all of which can be expected to be terminal.[89] Thus, the necessity for this type of training exists.

In view of this, the health care team, and in particular the physician, is still not receiving the proper orientation to work with the dying child. Most physicians receive their greatest amount of gratification from treatment success, their achievements being measured by the rehabilitation and restoration of the patients' health. When confronted with the dying child, the physician may believe he or she has little to offer and may become unavailable for continuous treatment. The matter is even worse when the physician continues to treat the child until the last minute of life, believing that everything should be done medically until the time of death.[90]

Last-minute heroics usually are not what is called for. Rather, the health care staff, as well as the family, should be concerned with making sure the child is comfortable when dying. Extremely important in achieving this goal is proper management of pain medication for the dying child. There is no reason why any child, especially the terminally ill child, should be in pain. No effective medication should be withheld. Often both the physician and nurse need to be reminded and supported in this regard, though they may hesitate to deviate from the standard dose and its usual applications.[91] To be able to institute successful pain control at home, the physician needs to allow the nurse and family flexibility in pain management. This can be done by prescribing a wide range of doses.[92]

Although some people may still look upon home care for the dying child with pessimism, there are appreciable benefits. The family and child who decide on home care seem to be better adjusted to the child's fate. These psychological and social benefits stem from the environment of love and security that the home provides. By providing these comforts, it helps promote the honesty and openness that is truly needed by the dying child. At home, the child gets the attention and love that is so often lacking in the hospital. The family's desires to actively participate in the care of their child are also better fulfilled. And all these advantages—improved satisfaction with the environment and the health care delivered—are available at a reduced financial cost.

7

The Dying Adolescent

> *I know it's all too late in coming . . .*
> *But . . . there were always things*
> *I meant to say . . .*
> *Things I always thought we'd share*
> *Later . . .*
> *When we were old . . .*
> —Merrit Malloy

Dying is never an easy process; neither is growing up. The death of a young person always seems more tragic than that of an older person. Dying for a very young child is difficult in the sense that it is hard to understand what is occurring, but dying for an adolescent, a person just beginning to live an adult life, may be the most difficult of all. The mere process of adolescence can be traumatic enough without having to face the possibility of its cessation. This is what prompted Adele Hofmann to state, "From so many aspects, dying teenagers are the greatest mourners of their own fate."[93]

According to Piaget, adolescence is the age at which people take their place in adult society, and thus, he maintains it is the age of the formation of the personality. This is the point in people's lives when they are planning for themselves a life program and generally have many plans of change, not only for themselves, but also for the world around them. Adolescents are arranging their scale of values, placing some ideals above others toward their life goals. The life plan of adolescents is also their assertion of autonomy and indicates their willingness to plunge into adult life, as well as their image of themselves as the equal of adults.

June Jackson Christmas, M.D. delineates the four major tasks a person faces during adolescence. The first task is to develop a psychosexual identity. This is often complicated by adolescents' varying views of social behavior, as well as that of their parents and their peers. The varying ideologies proposed by society and the media further complicate this issue. The second task is to resolve the conflicts related to dependence and independence. This age is a difficult transition from childhood to adulthood. The adolescent may be treated alternately as a child and an adult, and thus, displays rapidly changing behavior—one moment needing to be cared for and nurtured, the next appearing assertively and aggressively "adult." The third task, the development of a system of values, is a complicated and stressful procedure in which young people are torn between the values of their peers and those of their parents, while observing a society in which moral values often appear to be little more than empty words. Finally, the adolescent's fourth task is the choice of vocational goals. In today's society, where rapidly advancing technology has made this a complicated task, options are quite varied, but limitations are rife. Along with, and closely related to, the psychological development of the adolescent is the physical development. Puberty marks the onset of adolescence. Puberty is signified in boys by an increase in testicular size as spermatogenesis begins. Later signs are growth in size of the penis and scrotum and the presence of thick, curly pubic hair. In girls the first sign of puberty is the appearance of the breast bud. This is followed by the growth of sparse hair along the medial edges of the labia. After this time, menarche occurs, and breast development continues throughout puberty. Although the outward sex organ changes are the prime indicators of puberty, there are multiple changes occurring in an adolescent's body. Adolescent males grow rapidly in height and weight, their voices change, they develop facial hair, and many other hormonally mediated events occur. In females, there are marked outward bodily changes accompanying menstruation and breast development. Because of these bodily changes, adolescence is a period of marked narcissicism.

Adolescence is a period of great turmoil physically, psychologically, and socially. Adolescents have passed the stage of viewing death as temporary, and their ideas approximate those of adults. Young persons have come to perceive the reality, totality, and finality of death. Although adolescents fully comprehend the irreversible nature of psychological death, it is during this time of uncompromised idealism and search for values and ethics that they may invest death with some sort of spiritual continuation.

The primary causes of death during adolescence are accidents, suicides, and malignancies. The first two leave the survivors shocked and numb; they are generally quick and have no aftereffect on the adolescent. Malignancies and other terminal illnesses are another issue completely. "Even if a patient does believe in afterlife, the impact of dying, with all its deteriorating functions, is particularly difficult for an adolescent to bear."[94] Young people, just at the point of achieving adult status, and what they perceive to be the freedom of action and choice, are acutely aware that their impending death means the loss of everything. The adolescent's loss of control and independence, consequences of serious illness, also create problems in the dying adolescent, as does the deterioration of physical and sexual integrity brought about by illness and chemical and surgical interventions. Another point that must be addressed is the legal aspects of these cases; many youths are capable of forming opinions and making decisions, but legally they are still subject to parental decisions. Although each case must be treated individually according to the maturity of the given adolescent, such questions as "Should they be told their diagnosis?" "Should they be asked to consent to mutilative surgical procedures?" "Do they have the full confidentiality in the patient-doctor relationships?" must be answered.

The psychological problems displayed by the dying adolescent fall into four general categories: alteration of self-concept, alteration of body image, difficulty in interpersonal relationships, and interference with future plans. Specific problems include loss of self-esteem, loss of hair, loss of an extremity, difficulty with friends and family, and questions about career education, marriage, and death. When adolescents first learn their diagnosis, they undergo an alteration of self-concept. At an age when belonging is very important, the knowledge that they have a disease that requires long-term treatment causes a feeling of inferiority and a loss of self-esteem. Their immediate concerns are not about the possibility of death, but about how the disease will make them different from others their age. Adolescents frequently wonder how their friends will treat them and whether or not they will be rejected. Because of this, adolescents will often go to great lengths to conceal their disease. One case history, discussed in "Psychological Problems in Adolescents with Malignancy" notes that C.M., a twenty-year-old girl with stage-four Hodgkin's disease failed to inform her prospective employer of her illness, thinking that if he knew he wouldn't hire her. Eventually, she decided to tell the man and was hired without reservation.[95] Although adolescents not only hide their disease from others, but try to hide it from themselves, the weekly or bi-weekly visits to the clinic are a reminder of their condition. Their feelings of weakness and inferiority increase as malaise, fatigue, and anorexia force them to limit their activities. Another case discussed in the article mentioned above concerns J.L., an eighteen-year-old boy with stage-three Hodgkin's disease who had been a star basketball player until his illness. He claimed everyone would know something was wrong and dropped out of school. After assurance that when he felt better he could continue to participate in his normal activities, J.L. returned to school and graduated with his class. Since some chemotherapeutic agents produce nausea and vomiting the day after administration, some adolescent students may not wish to attend class following therapy. Students who do attend class may appear less interested, and an insensitive teacher may complain and increase the adolescent's feelings of inferiority and lowered self-esteem.

The second major problem encountered by adolescents with a

malignancy is alteration in body image. Since adolescents' images of their own bodies undergo rapid change as the body matures physiologically, any change secondary to therapy only complicates their adjustment to this change. One example of a complication of therapy is alopecia, the loss of one's hair due to chemotherapeutic agents and sometimes radiation therapy. The loss of hair immediately marks both boys and girls as different and may be viewed as more bothersome than the disease itself. To girls it means loss of attractiveness and femininity; to boys loss of sex appeal and virility. Although wigs may be used to disguise this problem, it can be difficult to keep hair loss secret, and for some adolescents it is very embarrassing for anyone to know they wear a wig. Radiation dermatitis can also be a problem because, not only does the skin appear flaky and darkened, but these teenagers must be excluded from outdoor swimming and sun bathing. A more drastic alteration in body image occurs in patients who have lost a limb. The fear of unacceptability and isolation secondary to disfigurement can be a much greater source of anxiety than the fear of death itself, or recurrence of cancer. There are some patients who would rather die than be severely disfigured. Many adolescents, after the initial period of mourning for the limb and subsequent loss of self-esteem, adjust outwardly quite well, but there is no information about their behavior at home and elsewhere.

Another problem encountered in adolescent patients with malignancies is the difficulty in managing interpersonal relationships. Normal adolescents generally have some difficulty with interpersonal relationships because of their struggle between dependence and independence, which is intensified in the adolescent with cancer. They may interpret their forced dependence on their parents and physician as weakness. Fear of rejection is very intense in adolescents with cancer. Not only will they be burdened with the thoughtless remarks of peers as to their differences, but they may also be subjected to the oversympathetic, solicitous attitudes of parents and peers. They wish very much to be treated like everyone else. Although their peers react this way out of fear and sympathy, it is difficult for adolescents with cancer to appreciate these efforts, which further complicates matters. It will probably be necessary for ill adolescents to educate their peers as to the nature of their disease, and thus allow relationships to be established on an altered but more normal basis. Overprotective parents may also pose problems. The gifts and favors they bestow on the ill adolescent may help alleviate their fear and guilt, but they place the adolescent back into an independence-dependence struggle. The physician-adolescent relationship is also very important. The physician must be trustworthy and honest with the adolescent patient, but at the same time try not to frighten or depress the youth. The physician must also spend time talking and listening to the adolescent on an adult-to-adult basis.

Finally, there is the problem of adolescents' questions about the future. Adolescents with cancer will ask questions about a future career, education, marriage, and death. Generally, adolescents who have adjusted well to their illness are encouraged to make plans for a realistic future, with the understanding that these may be interrupted at some future time for treatment of the disease. Many adolescents, especially girls, wonder about the possibility of marriage as they watch their friends marrying and beginning families. It is sometimes necessary for a female with lesions in the pelvis to receive local irradiation, which results in sterility. Also, many drugs given to combat cancer are teratogenic, and pregnancy is ruled out in these cases. Loss of reproductive ability indicates loss of femininity in these females and results in further alteration of self-concept. Adolescents' first questions about death may come upon hearing the diagnosis, but when in remission or feeling well, they may forget this possibility. The next realization that death is near may come with a relapse or when adolescents realize their condition is not improving. Although the adolescents are struggling to be independent, impending death may be too great an anxiety for them to cope with, bringing about depression or regression to childlike states, both of which involve withdrawal of emotional energy from life. There may also be rage, usually directed at themselves for being so weak and imperfect that they cannot direct their lives to fulfillment.

Guilt may also be present in dying adolescents. Since adolescence is normally a time for emancipation and testing of limits of one's freedom, death may be viewed as due punishment for sins they feel they have committed. During the time of approaching death, it is vital that physicians do not merely view this situation as a failure and therefore avoid it. Not only should they make sure the patient is receiving proper palliation and pain relief, but they should show the same concern, reassurance, and sympathetic ear that were offered earlier in the illness as an integral part of total care.

There are numerous case histories that illustrate a triphasic response by adolescents to their impending death. Kübler-Ross's five stages—denial of the fact that death is near, anger over being the victim, a bargaining for more time, depression and grief over expected losses, and acceptance that one's time has come—have been modified by Reich and Feinberg to more closely fit the adolescent's response. The first phase is characterized by anxiety and depression, with a withdrawal of emotional energy from life itself. The second phase is one of motor activity, which they feel represents a return to an earlier developmental pattern whereby tension and anxiety are relieved through motor discharge. This phase is also seen as a denial of increasing immobility and the gradual onset of death. The third phase is a regression to an earlier developmental period, when mother is all-powerful and touch and closeness bring relief from anxiety, even the pain of death.

It is impossible to fully understand the scope of the problem of dying adolescents without also dealing briefly with family members. The feelings displayed by family members very closely resemble the pattern delineated by Kübler-Ross of dying people and their families, although the family deals with the dying adolescent basically in the same manner as they would a younger child with a few differences, noted in the book *The Hospitalized Adolescent*. Since teenagers have begun, through various degrees of alienating and confrontational behavior, to emancipate themselves from their parents and family, they may find it distressing to be forced into a dependent situation. This is a time in which, more than ever, adolescents need the caring of their mother and father, and they face special problems in understanding and meeting these conflicts. The first reaction of parents faced with the prospect that their child is dying is one of shock and disbelief. They may openly admit that they do not want to believe the diagnosis and may continue to deny the reality as long as possible. As a consequence of this denial, the parents may take the ill child from doctor to doctor seeking a more hopeful diagnosis. Although this can be carried to excess, it is therapeutic for the parents to at least obtain a second or third diagnosis to reassure themselves that they have done everything possible for the child. As the parents begin to face the reality of the impending death, they anticipate the loss of a relationship that has been extremely meaningful. In facing this loss, they may become very sad and show little energy in day-to-day tasks. Even though the family members are sad, they usually are not depressed. Depression is marked by a loss of self-esteem, and in realization of the care and help they can give this dying child, they may achieve a deeper feeling of self-worth.

Guilt again plays a very large part in the family reaction. Mothers and fathers berate themselves for not noticing the symptoms earlier, and brothers and sisters may feel guilty that they were not better protectors. Very often the family's anger may be vented toward the physician and other members of the caring team. The treatment team must realize that this anger may be merely an integral part of the mourning process. As part of the mourning process, family members must begin to reinvest emotionally. They must begin to change their goals and their plans. They must start to rearrange the family constellation. Although this is very important, in some families the parents and relatives may abruptly withdraw their emotional investments from the child, and the child becomes isolated and alone. This can sometimes occur almost as an agreement between the family and the dying child. Most children care deeply for their families and do not wish to cause them pain. They will therefore encourage their parents and family members to drift away emotionally, so as not to hurt them.

Although parents may be anxious and fearful about the hospitalization of a child, they also may be eager for the child to be placed in a situation where they can deny the possibility that the child may die and develop unreasonable hopes for a cure to be received in the hospital. The family may also be very apprehensive when the child has a symptomatic remission and is allowed to return home. They fear they will be unable to cope with the child, and they fear they may hurt the child in some way. The mother bears the greatest burden of these family fears, and she may become so overprotective that she isolates the child. During the child's illness and after death, the sorrowing family is expected to be depressed and withdrawn according to social customs. If the mother wears an especially colorful dress to cheer herself, or the father attempts to relieve his tensions through a golf game, or a brother or sister appears too cheerful, they may be labeled socially bad. This enforced isolation may become almost unbearable, and the family members can hardly avoid blaming the child for having made their lives so difficult. Although each family and each situation is unique, this is always a stressful and complicated process to undergo.

Physicians and all members of the treatment team undergo many of the same reactions the family members do in dealing with dying children or adolescents. In dealing with adolescents, physicians must realize that they are dealing with people who usually are more adult than child. Communication is the key in the treatment of dying adolescents. Not only should the adolescents have treatments and procedures explained to them, but they should be listened to by physicians. Physicians should not only answer academic questions, but they should listen to and help the adolescents deal with their feelings. Physicians, like many people, strive to maintain a comfortable distance from the realities of death. The approaching death of children or adolescents places a great emotional burden on doctors, and they will deal with this stress as they have dealt with stress in the past. This may come in the form of worrying, compulsion, or intellectualization. Like the family, doctors have an emotional investment in the child, and must go through a mourning process.

They must also go through emotional reinvestment, and like the family, must guard against doing this before the death of the child. It is important that physicians don't view the impending death as a failure, and therefore withdraw from the child or adolescent, feeling there is nothing else they can do. It is vital that they provide, especially to the adolescent, the caring and understanding that they did throughout the illness.

Although the case of the dying adolescent is a truly complex problem, through teamwork between the treatment team, the family, and the adolescent, many of the problems can be thwarted with caring, listening, and understanding.

8

Parental Guilt and Grief

*"You can't prevent birds of sorrow
from flying over your head—but you can prevent them
from building nests in your hair."*
—ancient Chinese proverb

Unfortunately, many parents who have lost children let their nests grow very large. Bereavement, to parents, is a shattering of their world, a violation of natural law: the parents have outlived their child. No longer will they be able to muse about the future of their progeny, or wonder what color their grandchildren's eyes will be. Walks in the park, first dates, the shine in the child's eyes when opening a birthday present—none of this will happen again. Never. Death will inevitably mean a change in life style for the parents, regardless of their age or the amount of time separated from the child. A great-grandmother in her eighties can grieve for her lost daughter with the same severity as can a young parent mourning the death of an infant.

The change in life style can result in destruction of a parent's previous relationships and further family crises. Drunkenness, separation, divorce, and social alienation are frequently the aftermath of a child's death. A continuum of psychological and behavioral symptoms also follows in the wake of bereavement; they include somatic distress, such as diminished appetite, insomnia, and nausea; preoccupation with the image of the deceased; hostile reactions; loss of patterns of conduct; social alienation; and guilt, the most tormenting accompaniment of death. But why would parents implicate themselves in the death of their child? The answer is not simple; guilt is a complex phenomenon, involving hostility, powerlessness, and religion.

Guilt. According to Robert J. Lifton, it is, in the psychological sense, "an individual sense of badness or evil, with a fear or expectation of punishment," and it is experienced "when one feels responsible, through action or inaction, for separation, stress, or disintegration."[96] In grieving parents, this reaction is pathognomonic for their situation. They search the period of time before their child's death for any small indication of failure to meet the child's needs, accusing themselves of gross negligence and exaggerating any omission they might find in their care of the child. Frequently, they irrationally conclude that some unrelated incident caused that fatal illness, as in the case of one mother who was convinced that her daughter had "caught" leukemia from the tumor of a family pet. She felt she might have been able to prevent the illness had she removed the animal from the household.

Another manifestation of parental guilt uses God as a mediator; some parents consider that the child's death is an act of retribution by God for some trangression that they feel they might have committed, from an infrequent church-attendance record to marital infidelity. Following the death of a son from leukemia, a father fears his son's illness was punishment for his marital infidelity.

Through psychoanalysis, we learn that guilt can arise from a number of causes. Freud pioneered the idea that guilt springs from hostility. In his paper "Mourning and Melancholia," Freud theorizes that because all close relationships are characterized by ambivalence—feelings of both love and hate—the loss of a loved one creates an unconscious sense of guilt. Since we don't want to hate the person who has just died, we hate ourselves instead, and this leads to depression and guilt. Elisabeth Kübler-Ross agrees that anger can be a contributor to a survivor's guilt, for relatives are often guilt-ridden because of angry wishes toward the dead person. And who, in anger, has not at times wished someone would "drop dead"?[97] These hostile sentiments may seem to indicate to grieving parents that they hadn't loved the child enough, or in the "right" way—and these sentiments are the basis for intense self-blame. The parents long for someone to blame, for some way to avenge their child's death. When parents find a presumed discrepancy in their treatment of the child, they turn their anger at the child's death in on themselves and collapse into a morass of grief.

More recently, psychoanalyst Melanie Klein believed that the adult guilt stemmed from a regression to the behavior of childhood. She said that bereaved adults become like children who have lost something precious to them. They protest by grieving and blame themselves for the loss; they must have done something wrong to have had their child taken away.

A third explanation for the causation of guilt comes from Colin Murray Parkes, who believes that self-blame is a means for the bereaved to feel they have some control over the circumstances of the death of their child. Says Parkes:

> The death of a loved person is so important an event that it is difficult to shrug it off as the result of an accident or ill luck. Untimely deaths cast doubt upon the reasonable expectations upon which all of us base our lives. We know that disasters happen but we cannot afford to worry about disasters which are statistically unlikely . . . to worry about the possibilities would make life intolerable, and most people rely on the knowledge that accidents are statistically rare, and feel that they are protected from disaster. A major bereavement shakes confidence in the sense of security. The tendency to go over the events leading up to the loss and to find someone to blame, even if it means accepting the blame oneself is a less disturbing alternative than accepting that life is uncertain. If we can find someone to blame, or some explanation that will enable death to be evaded, then we have a chance on controlling things.[98]

Self-blame affords a handle with which bereaved parents can retain a grasp on their lives and that of their families. To the parent in grief, this lack of control is intolerable—powerlessness to protect offspring is contradictory to basic parental instincts. This powerlessness is described in an old Syrian legend:

A beautiful youth, the son of the sultan, dashed into his father's palace in Damascus crying that he had to leave immediately for Baghdad. When the sultan asked the lad why he was in such haste, the boy replied, "I just saw Death standing in the palace garden, and when he saw me, he stretched out his arms as if to threaten me. I must lose no time in escaping him." Agreeing, the sultan gave the boy his swiftest horse. When he left, the ruler angrily stalked into his garden and demanded to know of Death how he dared to intimidate the son of a sultan. Death listened, astonished, and answered, "I assure you I did not threaten your son. I only threw up my arms in surprise at seeing him here because I have a rendezvous with him tonight in Baghdad."[99]

The sultan, despite his apparent power, had no control over the destiny of his son. He was able to realize the hopelessness of trying to change the situation; most parents, however, too often believe they should have been able to avert the tragedy of their child's death. They search the past in an attempt to find a cause for this calamity. One father, the parent of a leukemic child, said, "If there were a reasonable explanation, anything that would explain this a little, I could accept it and live with it a little better." This process of assuming responsibility and guilt brings a measure of relief. Parents, accepting guilt, can deny the unacceptable conclusion that no one is responsible for their child's death, and therefore that neither repentance nor self-punishment can undo the fated event, which killed without meaning.

Sometimes, the belief in self-guilt can become so strong in parents that they actually confess to the purported murder of the child. One mother confessed to the murder of her child and could not rid herself of self-blame, even though the coroner's report showed the baby had died of infant-death syndrome. Acquitted by courts, she still could not acquit herself.

R.A. Gardner feels that this necessity for personal control over calamity is based on love and affection, rather than on the hostility frequently described in Freud's works. He believes that parental guilt and desire for control stem from the wish to see the fatal illness undone or prevented in the future. Rollo May, in *The Meaning of*

Anxiety, writes, "If the disease were an accident, how could they be certain it would not occur again and again? If, on the other hand, the patient feels that his own pattern of life was at fault . . . he feels more guilt, to be sure, but at the same time he sees more hopefully what conditions need to be corrected to overcome his disease."[100]

A study was done to observe the components of the guilt affecting parents of children with severe physical disease. The researcher found at the outset that the parental guilt reaction was not related to the nature of the child's disease. He conducted interviews with all parents, structured so that the parents would not realize that the primary focus of the interview was the guilt reaction, and thus they would answer truthfully rather than in a way they deemed correct. He then developed a scale that evaluated the relative degree of love and hostility the parents felt toward their child. Parents whose affection dominated over their hostility obtained a high score. Other indices measured were conscious awareness, intrafamilial relationships, hostility inhibition, and magic thinking. Of the ten parents in the study judged to exhibit an inappropriate guilt reaction (so judged by the researcher), five could not be explained by either the anger/ hostility or the affection theories, two were found to exhibit Freudian hostility (they received scores of -3 and $+6$ out of a possible 32 points), and three parents' guilt was judged to be due to affection/need for control (they received scores of $+12$, $+21$, and $+32$).

In all five parents showing a definite guilt pattern, a variable called "magical thinking" was at work. To them, the disease of their child represented somehow the magical fulfillment of their wishes, whether hostile or affectionate. Since parents cannot control the situation by any earthly means, they resort to another alternative: magic. Under this category falls religon.

Religion offers the bereaved a means of adjustment to the stressful reality. No longer do parents have to say, "I don't know why." Now they can say, "God did it because I failed." Parents are thus relieved of the intolerable state of having no control over their family's welfare; they have found a reason for the child's death. To many parents, this reason, once found, is a source of comfort:

something tangible to deal with. Religion, too, serves the purpose of providing a means of atoning for the guilt a parent feels.

Many philosophers feel that a fear of death is instilled by religion. In the Bible, death is called "the enemy": "The last enemy to be abolished is death" (1 Cor. 15:26); and "In the days of His flesh, He offered both prayers and supplication with loud crying and tears to the One able to save Him from death . . . " (Rom. 5:12). In the eleventh century, a writer called Anselm expressed the essence of Christian (and Judean) thought about death in *Cur Deus Homo*: it is seen as a sin-induced intrusion into the order of life.

With the concept that death is the result of sin, then, parents have found a reason for their child's death; namely, that they, the parents, have done something wrong, and that they are being punished for their transgression by God. This idea of heavenly punishment is evident in all denominations of Christian faith. In a study by Glenn Vernon, a questionnaire sampling the connection between religious affiliation and attitudes toward death asked the question "Have you ever had a feeling of being punished by God for something you have done?"[101] The following results were obtained.

Denomination	I'm sure I have	I think I have	No	No answer
Independent	7.1*	16.5	77.9	3.5
Episcopalian	11.0	42.5	45.2	1.4
Congregational	15.9	42.8	40.4	1.0
Methodist	18.6	43.5	36.1	1.5
Presbyterian	22.9	40.0	37.1	
Lutheran	29.3	46.6	24.1	
Protestant	30.2	20.9	46.5	2.3
Catholic	30.7	42.1	26.0	.9
Mormon	31.3	30.5	37.8	.4
Baptist	33.7	39.8	26.0	.6
Jewish	38.7	41.3	17.3	2.0

This data indicates that those who are members of strongly direc-

*The results are all expressed in percentages.

tive denominations, such as Catholicism, Judaism, Baptist, and Mormonism, all see God as a deliverer of punishment, whereas people independent from a church do not see punishment from God as a means of expiating sins. Perhaps religion, in this context, offers to those persons who feel guilty for something they might have done a method of atoning for, and thus partially removing, the guilt.

Religion can be involved in parental guilt in other ways. One mother, who believed strongly that God controls the lives of his progeny on earth, thought that through her prayers she manipulated the fate of her child. When having marital troubles, she prayed for "something to open my husband's eyes" to divert him from quarreling: "Maybe I'm too religious, but I prayed to God to send something to open my husband's eyes. Right after that L. got sick. . . . I figured that one of the children would get sick, and he would get so interested in the child that he would forget about this." Some time after her prayer, her son was diagnosed as having leukemia. Her belief in the efficacy of prayer extended to her son's eventual death. After the son's illness had progressed for several months, her husband asked her to pray for his death as a means to release him from further suffering. She believed that her prayers determined the time of her son's death. "I always prayed that my son would live and my husband believed that everything I prayed for happened. But that Saturday he said that I should pray for the opposite—that I should pray for my son to die so he shouldn't suffer anymore. I did pray for him to die, but I didn't really mean it and it seemed that it happened just one, two, three when nobody expected it. I know that it was going to happen because I had prayed for it. I prayed that it should happen without any suffering and it happened exactly that way."[102] In this case, too, one wonders if the parent would have found herself responsible for her child's death had she not had such faith in the power of God's omnipotence.

If religion offers a pathway to self-blame for bereaved parents, it also offers the social support necessary to rid the parent of that guilt. Clergy will visit the grieving parents, visiting whenever they feel needed; lay people are quick to come by with offerings of food, companionship, and social stimulation. An explanation of the guilt suffered by the parents is readily offered by most ministers, which may provide some comfort:

> We also recognize that the burden of guilt hangs heavily upon us, for we know that we are interrelated and interdependent, and when something ill happens to one, it in a measure happens to all. But we also know that our feelings here are the sign both of our burden and of our salvation, for it takes a highly developed moral sensitivity to be aware of the burden and to carry it with courage. Just as grief is the other side of the coin of love, so feelings of guilt are the other side of the coin of moral responsibility.
>
> There is the guilt that we can relieve by the acts of restitution. We can do good to another for the injury we have done. We can pay the debt with interest. We can ask and receive forgiveness. This is the normal way for us to meet the burdens of real guilt. This is the way of the Lord's Prayer, with its recognition of the reciprocal relationship between failure and forgiveness: forgive as we forgive. But when death intervenes, and we cannot do the acts of restitution directly, what then? We use our feelings to build up that reservoir of right relationships and goodwill from which humankind draws its needed supply of understanding and kindliness. The good that we would have done another, and cannot, can become the good that we would do in this person's name. In this way even our being becomes a living memorial.[103]

The role of religion, then, in the expression of guilt in bereaved parents, is in offering parents an outlet for, and a means of dealing with, their guilt. Since the phenomenon of self-blame is noted universally as a symptom of grief, and not just among those admitting religious preference, it is unlikely that the imposition of religious mores (a set of rules to break) is the sole contributor to the roots of this phenomenon; anger, hostility, and powerlessness seem to play as big a part. Whatever the cause, guilt remains a painful addition to the loss of a child, the loss of future joys. The main task of bereaved parents is to admit their humility, to admit that they had no power over the death of their progeny. Once reconciled, they must go on with life, realizing that the emptiness is going to be there always, but that so, too, will the joys. If their church can help them to do this, then it is a valuable relationship.

There will always be memories and pain. But the important thing is to enjoy those memories—and resume life.

> *His little arms crept 'round my neck*
> *And then I heard him say*
> *Four simple words I shan't forget*
> *Four words that made me pray...*
> *They turned a mirror on my soul*
> *On secrets no one knew.*
> *They startled me, I hear them yet;*
> *He said, "I'll be like you."*
>
> —Herbert Parker

9

Coping with Death:
Teacher and Child

Most teachers at some time will have to deal with the painful experience of helping a child in their class cope with the death of a family member or friend. The quality of the child's interaction with adults is one of the vital factors that determines how well they will cope with death. Because teachers are vital adults in the lives of the children in their classrooms, it is essential that they learn how to help children cope with death. Hawener and Phillips also state that if teachers and counselors are to be helpful to children, it is important that they reexamine and come to terms with their own values and beliefs regarding death.[104] The psychological effects of death on children can be long lasting. Consequently, death should be emphasized more in the primary and secondary educational curriculums. This education could be extremely beneficial if presented informatively and straightforwardly. Teachers can have a great impact on how children see death, because the first thing presented to students is the teacher's experience with death. It is important for teachers to know where a child is in regard to their own level of thinking. Children go through the grief cycle much differently than adults do.

We must expose children to the fact that death is very natural, something that happens to everyone. Grade-school children are particularly interesting to me. This is a time of great vulnerability and innocence. It is a very crucial period concerning a child's curiosity with death and dying. This chapter will focus on children in the seven-to-nine age group. Behavior symptoms and problems that are psychological, physical, and social in nature will be discussed. Solutions and recommendations for the teacher are also an important part of the process in dealing with the grieving child.

In children aged seven to nine, death is understood as final, but personified as a skeleton, bogeyman, or otherwise. The personification is external, so death can be escaped by running away or hiding by recitation of magical formulas. Children of this age do not commonly express their grief verbally, but speak to us in symbolic language, using fantasy play or acting out feelings for which they have no words.

A teacher should try to identify the uncharacteristic behavior for a child and for the developmental stage of that child. Any marked change is enough to suspect that it is a grief response. Grief is more apt to be worked out in the child's behavior. Some reactions to grief are those of hostility, guilt, fear, and displacement.

They will show grief through anger. They feel deprived of something important in their lives, and because they cannot understand what has happened, they relate their feelings to the rest of their experience.[105] Hostile feelings result from the feeling of being left or separated from the loved one. Children often feel that the death was a result of their misbehavior. This often leads to the child's misbehavior in the classroom.

Another common feeling is one of guilt. Grieving children often feel guilty when a parent or loved one dies. Guilt plays an important role in grieving. However, with children it is often egocentric in nature. Their capacity for grasping enlarged ideas has not fully developed. Ideas are still focused upon themselves, their lives, their feelings. For example, when the father of an eight-year-old boy dies, the child's grief is centered about an unfinished racing car he and his father were making.[106] In anger, at some point, children may have wished the death of the now deceased. When death occurs, they feel it is their fault. Children who have said "I wish you were dead" do not know the full meaning of their words, but they may well be overwhelmed by their feelings about the magical power of their words if, shortly thereafter, that adult should die. They quite naturally feel that it is their fault.[107]

Fear is also present when a child is grieving. "Who will be next?" Fear derived from the tentativeness and fragility of life is an extremely natural feeling.[108] Teachers need to explore these fears with the child and must, therefore, be in touch with their own feelings. Ages seven to nine is when a realistic conception takes place, namely death as a permanent biological process. They cannot yet differentiate between wish and deed, and there may be a great deal of remorse.

Children who are not permitted to show feelings of grief over the loss of something or someone important to them have no choice other than to fall back on more primitive measures of defense, most often the denial of the pain of loss. Children have a right to grieve without apology or shame.

Teachers should be aware of the possibility of a change of interest in grieving children. Many display their grief by displacing their feelings in other situations. School is a main focus for such displacement. Activities that once interested such children are abandoned. Grieving children need a supportive adult who will help them find new reasons for continuing to learn and play. Some of the symptoms one should be aware of are:

1. The child cannot concentrate on schoolwork.
2. The child has no desire to play with friends.
3. The child is antisocial and despondent.[109]

Psychological, physical, and social problems are common to children in terms of death and dying. Grieving children experience obvious deficits in their ability to cope. It is very important that a child is noticed. Teacher's efforts with the grieving child are of great importance. They spend a great deal of time with the child, and their perception of the situation, and ways of dealing with it, are very important.

Psychologically, the child is having a very hard time. There is really no way to prepare psychologically for the loss of a loved one. Studies have shown that when the subject of death is not handled well by adults, the child may be deeply injured. Often this shows itself by what is said, as well as by what is done.

Circumstances of the death and what preceded it must be considered. By age seven, children's perceptions of death have grown quite clear, and they show curiosity as to the causes. In addition, children have their first inkling that "I" may die, which should prompt calm assurance from the teachers. It is very important to make children understand that they are entitled to have and express feelings, and that it would be wrong and perhaps harmful not to do so.

At ages seven to nine, children see death as occurring mostly to the old, but they are beginning to sense that it can occur to adults like their parents and possibly even to children like themselves.[110]

A teacher should note that the child may lapse into long periods of apprehensiveness. The child must realize that weeping is okay and very healthy. Make the child understand that crying is for the one who will be missed so much. A seven- to nine-year-old still has a limited vocabulary for use during stressful situations, and it is good to release these intense feelings.

Children will often have violent outbursts accompanied by tears. They may seem to be in a dazed withdrawal and often this internalization will lead to physical ailments or collapse.

Social isolation is another common problem. Searching is a very common reaction to death. The task of testing reality has started. Children will often find it hard to believe their loss and will search for the absent object. In the process, they will have shut out any outside contacts.

Teachers should be aware of their students' willingness to discuss their feelings in the classroom. They should consider the social maturity of the student. Facing the reality of death may lead to overwhelming anxiety for a particular student. To cope, the individual may use avoidance behavior toward the denial of death. A teacher who sees this should not try to eradicate this coping pattern.

Shakespeare has Hamlet's mother say, "Thou know'st 'tis common, all that live must die." It is equally common, therefore, that bereavement through death has to be faced as a fact of life. Yet however honestly it is faced, bereavement brings about a crisis of loss, probably the most severe crisis in human existence.[111] In this situation of inevitability and crisis, what help does the bereaved need and what help can be offered?

Most researchers agree that honesty is essential when discussing death with children. It is also very important to use direct language when discussing death. Many children suffer because adults try to soften the reality with euphemisms. "She's gone away." "Daddy's in heaven." "He's gone to sleep forever." The use of such terminology with young people serves only to perpetuate the confusion that these sort of words can hold. The teacher can greatly aid a child who is grieving by just being a friend, a friend who will listen and honestly answer questions. The teacher can help children work through their feelings.

Mental health depends upon the frank acknowledgment of the denial of tragedy. Thinking and talking about death need not be morbid. Ignorance and fear of death overshadow the life, while knowing about and accepting death erases this shadow. Most studies have found that it is more helpful to permit young children to inquire about death, to share memories, observations, and feelings with adults in response to the death of a significant person.[112]

Questions should be answered honestly or not at all. Honest responses convey all the emotions from the sadness of loss to happy memories and remembrance of the joy that person brought into our lives. Holding children when they need to express their grief is a genuine act; children need to feel love and caring when they must face the loss of a well-loved person. Talking, silence, and tears, each in their time, may be therapeutic.

Children should be encouraged to express what they feel, as opposed to being told how they should feel or act. Further, they also need to know that adults in their lives grieve; this may be the best basis for accepting their feelings as natural. It is important for children to know that it is okay for them to feel the way they do. It is crucial that the attitudes of teachers help in recovery from the crisis of loss.

All mourners need special sympathy and support from the people around them. Bowlby said that to tolerate separation anxiety and to mourn are signs of the healthy personality who is capable of deep attachment. Without real attachments, secure autonomy cannot be achieved.[113] Only when the lost person has been internalized and becomes part of the bereaved, a part that can be integrated with the bereaved's own personality and enrich it, is the mourning process complete.

Another issue a teacher must deal with is that of the other children in the class. The teacher can help the other children also in coping with death. When one child is grieving it affects the entire learning environment. Calvin Calarusso addresses this problem in his article "Johnny Did Your Mother Die?" It deals not only with Johnny, the grieving child, but also with his classmates. The teacher must also help the other children overcome their fears. In this article all the children reacted in some way to the death of Johnny's mother. Some children experienced anxiety over leaving their own mothers in the morning. Others' play became violent, usually involving death. The teacher assured these children (ages seven to eight) by explaining that none of their parents were expected to die soon. She also involved the other children in helping John deal with his grief. She talked with them about appreciating Johnny's feelings and being kind. By involving the class, not only did the teacher learn, but she also helped the other children deal with death.[114]

Children are curious about, and perhaps fearful of, a child with a life-threatening illness such as cancer. Teachers can do much to allay such fears and satisfy the curiosity of the class by their acceptance of the ill child and by facilitating a dialogue between the ill child and classmates. For example, noticing a child's hair loss through chemotherapy, students may ask, "What happened to your hair?" or, "How did you get sick?" "Will you get better?" and perhaps, "Could this happen to me?" Children and their teacher can learn much by such a dialogue: to accept the possibility of illness and death for everyone, and to see the child with a major illness as essentially the same as themselves.

Teachers should confront their own feelings and thoughts about death and death education. They should be good listeners and elicitors as well as skillful dispensers of information. What teachers say, how they say it, and how they strive to widen the understanding of students is of continual importance. Children should not feel that the adult is evading their questions.

Educators have a need for, and benefit from, a seminar on death. As long as there is life, there is death. They should be aware, knowledgeable, and able to help in dealing with death.

Statistics show that one out of five students will experience a parent's death during his or her school years.[115] Informal and formal death education should be developed and systematic. This should start in elementary school. Death education would:

1. foster better communication with loved ones
2. prepare one for subsequent events and consequences
3. be interventive and help a child presently facing an aspect of death
4. have a rehabilitative effect[116]

The changes we grieve as loss, as well as our grieving patterns themselves, are established in childhood. We have to teach children that loss is natural to life and that people and objects do not have permanence. A teacher should make it obvious that grief feelings are normal.

A reflective listener is very important to the welfare of the grieving child. One must realize that grief has its own unique rhythm and flow, which cannot be directed or contained by our willpower. Talking feelings out is one of the best cures.

Grief cannot be intellectualized away or thought through. Talking puts us in touch with our feelings. Time is the best healer.

It takes much living, thinking, and feeling to come to some

understanding about death. Everyone's reaction to and understanding of death is unique and personal.

In conclusion, I would like to stress that the teachers' greatest strength in helping a child cope with death is their own ability to cope. This, however, is not an easy task. It can be a valuable learning experience for those who choose to pursue the subject, and I feel it is a necessity. I have seen the problems of children who were inadequately dealt with after a death. Children, as all people, need love and a sense of security and empathy when trying to cope with the loss of a loved one. Teachers are in the ideal position to help children grow through this experience of grief.

10

Hospice Care
for the Dying Child
(Coauthored with Elisabeth Kübler-Ross, M.D.)

The hospice movement in the United States is making the process of dying easier and more humane for both terminally ill patients and their families. By integrating medical care with emotional and psychological care, home care with hospital or inpatient care, and family care with patient care, the hospice has evolved into a comprehensive program that attempts to meet the specific needs of the dying in every respect. Regular general hospitals are places one goes to for diagnosis, treatment, and cure—to recover from diseases, to be rid of various physical ailments. It is natural that patients are treated from the point of view of their illnesses; it is a matter of disease first, patient later, for as soon as the disease is done away with, the patient is restored to as close to normal as possible and can go on as before. Hospital and medical treatment is primarily geared toward the patient's future—and that is probably how it should, or must, be in our busy, impersonal society. But this is not the case with the dying. Since their future has been definitely limited, it is the present that is important. Since there is no more possibility for cure, emphasis must be placed on comfort and immediate symptom control. Since there is no returning to the past and to the normal way of life, primacy must be given to sincere individual attention and making the best of the given situation *now*. Dying is not a disease—its manifestations are not merely temporary and physical. Instead, dying affects every possible aspect of human existence; it is a physical, psychological, emotional, spiritual, and social process. Adequate treatment for the terminally ill must deal with this final and ultimate process of dying as a whole and not merely concentrate on one aspect alone. By incorporating multidisciplinary teams of various medical, health care, and social workers, hospices can give a patient total care where and when it is needed. The crucial distinction between the contexts, and more important, the needs of the normal hospital patient and the dying patient has been appreciated by hospices and acted upon to form methods and programs for better and more comprehensive care for the dying.

Hospice care attempts to

1. provide relief from distressing symptoms of the disease
2. provide the security of a caring environment
3. provide sustained expert medical and nursing care
4. provide assurance that patients and their families will not be abandoned

I shall not dwell anymore upon the goals, methods, and achievements of the hospice movement. The subject to be discussed is hospice care for the dying child. Hospices are a relatively new development in terminal care, especially in the United States where the few existent hospice programs are not more than three or four years old. Though we have one functioning children's hospice near Washington, D.C., and one being built in Salem, Oregon, the benefits of most hospice programs are limited to adults, those eighteen and older. But what about children with terminal illnesses; do they not also need the special comprehensive and individual care that a hospice organization could bring them? Admittedly, the needs of children and their families are different from and more varied than those of adults, and integrating child care into a regular hospice program could be quite difficult. However, it seems that children, too, and their families, should have the possibility of receiving adequate and intensive total terminal care, which can rarely be found in today's massive hospitals.

The term *child* covers such a wide range of stages in emotional, psychological, physical, social, and intellectual development that it is difficult to speak about the child as opposed to the adult. However, to generalize one could state that a child has not yet reached the levels of emotional, psychological, and intellectual maturity that are expected in most normal adults. Children's actual levels of development between the ages of birth and eighteen years will vary much more drastically than adults' levels between the ages of eighteen and ninety. Thus, children are less in control of their own situation in the world (the amount of control increasing with age) and are, to varying degrees, dependent on a parental or other adult figure (the degree of dependence decreasing with age). For the most part children are much more egocentric than adults, demanding and needing much more individual attention. Children have not learned to control the world around them as adults have, nor have they learned to conceptualize and objectify themselves and their situation. Again, these factors vary drastically with age and state of development. One must keep in mind that growth, change, and development are the very essence of childhood, and it is for this reason that it is much more complex than adulthood. Although the distinctions pointed out above between child and adult are simplistic indeed, even these play a significant role in determining the different relationships child and adult will have with impending death and the different methods of care needed to deal with each.

In the past, children were practically never actively involved in their own treatment. The past few years have shown a tremendous change in understanding the attitudes of dying children and have consequently altered the whole approach to the terminally ill child. The most significant changes originated in Switzerland approximately thirty years ago, with the revelation that children's spontaneous drawings reveal much of their inner knowledge and awareness of ill health and preconscious awareness of impending death. Dr. Elisabeth Kübler-Ross has used this method of spontaneous drawings with dying children over the last twenty years, and it can be used by any counselor, trained therapist, or physician in order to become more aware of children's inner knowledge of their terminal illness, as well as their prognosis. This knowledge, which can be obtained within ten minutes, has changed the entire approach to the dying child. We can now communicate with children in symbolic verbal and/or nonverbal language, which makes it possible for children to reveal their inner knowledge to the adults around them. The therapist or counselor acts as a catalyst and translator for the parents, facilitating communication between parent and child.

In most cases, when all medical means have been used and all medical-scientific resources have been depleted, the children ask to be allowed to go home. For example, children share verbally or nonverbally, in plain English or in symbolic language, whether they are willing or unwilling to continue chemotherapy. This is not just a reaction to the discomfort of treatment; it is also a result of their inner knowledge that further treatment will not produce further benefits. Children and parents should meet with the therapist, who understands the symbolic language of the child, to discuss the child's discharge from the hospital for either home or inpatient hospice care.

It seems self-evident that terminally ill children need and would benefit from hospice care as much as, if not more than, terminally ill adults. Children and their families' needs differ from those of adults in several respects, and a comprehensive program like that of a hospice could help fulfill those specific needs. First, children are not expected to take part (again depending on age and maturity) in the decision-making process of their own terminal care. It is usually the family of the child who takes the responsibility of decision-making, although the consequences will affect the child; thus a hospice's customary practice of regarding the patient and the family as a single unit of care would be especially beneficial in caring for the dying child. Since terminal illness in children is less frequent and seems more "unjust" than terminal illness in adults, families of young patients have even more difficulties in dealing with and accepting the situation. As Dr. Morris Green states, "There are few human experiences so shattering as a child's death." Therefore, the family would need trained emotional and psychological advice during, and most important, *after* the course of terminal illness. Another important point about children is that their reactions to their own impending death understandably vary greatly. The difference between the reactions and needs of two children of different ages or even the same age can be as great as that between child and adult. Therefore, an effective care program would require staff trained to deal with children not only on the medical level, but on psychological and emotional levels also. Because most children (depending on age and maturity) usually cannot be directly confronted with the fact of their own death, it is even more important that their daily lives retain as many aspects of their previous normal lives as possible. This, too, may put a greater burden on the parents, who may often feel the need to pretend that everything is all right with their child. Since the child is so dependent (depending on age) on the family and because of the need for a semblance of normality, it seems that, whenever possible, terminal care should take place in the home. Something like the hospice home care programs, with the addition of specially trained staff to meet the psychological and emotional needs of children of all ages, would appear to be the ideal answer to children's terminal care.

It is only in exceptional circumstances that home care is not sufficient at the end of a child's life. Inpatient hospice units can better serve those families with inadequate environments for home care, such as those with small, crowded quarters, those with many small children who also need care, those without an adult who could care for the dying child, or families with battered children. These relatively rare cases will require a hospice inpatient unit. These units are small set-ups and do not require separate buildings or administrations, which would make them economically unfeasible.

The palliative care unit of the Royal Victoria Hospital in Montreal is an example of an administrative compromise between a separate hospice unit and a regular ward within the framework of a children's hospital. These special palliative care units, or minihospice units, for children must have a totally independent staff with special awareness of the needs of their children. There must be rooms for parents, siblings of all ages, and grandparents, so that they can visit at any time of day or night. Ideally, these units should have adequate kitchen facilities where the family could prepare special meals, if necessary, for the dying child. There should be sleeping facilities with some privacy for the family, especially when the child is close to death. Adequate playrooms are also necessary, not only for visiting siblings, but for interaction between siblings and the terminally ill child. Additional facilities for supplying music are also important, especially for a terminally ill adolescent. Enough resource persons are needed, not only for the physical care of these children, but for their emotional, spiritual, and intellectual needs as well. These units could be run at economically reasonable rates and would not only benefit families with insufficient home care facilities, but would give families who are caring for their child at home a much-needed rest for a few weeks. This would allow parents to recuperate from home care and get a break when the terminal illness is of long duration.

The crucial and inherent bond between child and parent and the deep anxiety evoked in an adult by the dying child are two major factors that indicate the dire necessity to incorporate care for the family into the care given to the child. As Dr. Green points out, the dying child often awakens one of man's deepest fears—death before fulfillment.[117] The experience of a child's terminal illness probably causes more psychological and emotional problems in the family that is aware of the situation without being able to share it with the child (again, this depends on the age and maturity of the child).

The special needs of siblings of dying children must also be taken into consideration. They are often left out, while the dying child is spoiled with material things. Needless to say, these siblings grow extremely resentful, bitter, and jealous of the terminally ill child, though they would not change places. This kind of behavior is frequently observed and can be prevented by an understanding counselor who encourages the parents not to overreact to their terminally ill child. Large quantities of material things, which the terminally ill child neither needs nor really appreciates, do not relieve the parents of their sense of impotence.

Dr. Stanford B. Friedman points out what he feels to be most important in helping the family deal with its situation.[118] According to Friedman, physicians should be consciously aware of the common modes of adjustment used by parents, for only in this way will they be able to anticipate their needs, problems, and sources of anxiety. They should be able to give the parents emotional and psychological guidance and recognize the diverse forms of "coping behavior" that parents often manifest through denial. It is very important that doctors demonstrate their willingness to answer all the parents' questions, that they clearly discuss the disease with the parents, and that they explain the various possible courses the illness could take. The parents' participation in the child's care may also need to be guided; they may wish to stay with the child day and night in the hospital, or they may be reluctant to acknowledge how the child is feeling (denial). Parents will naturally impose their own fears or preconceptions of death on the child, and physicians should be aware of this while helping them do the most and best they can. They should also help the parents understand that it is common for such children to be angry that their parents cannot get rid of the pain and make them well. Finally, the relationship between the doctor and family should be a continuous one and not come to an end with the death of the child; as Friedman emphasizes, the physician can be of great help to parents months after the death of the child by going over issues or answering other related queries. The careful attention devoted to the family of the patient that Friedman advocates is similar to regular hospice procedures in caring for the terminally ill. Again, it seems that a hospice care program would be better equipped and coordinated to fulfill the needs of a dying child's family than the overburdened physician, who cannot be expected to be adequately trained in giving the psychological and emotional care and advice that is of foremost importance, or to go into the home and guide the family's treatment of the child.

Where one or two physicians alone cannot be expected to give comprehensive care and guidance to both patient and family in and out of the home, a hospice program could—and does—for adults. With few additions to the existing terminal care programs, hospices could guarantee to uphold the standards of care for dying children and their families put forth by Dr. Green and Dr. Friedman. The coordinated team of diversely trained staff, the care given to both patient and family together and individually, and the home care program so integral to hospices would be of infinite value to dying children and their parents. A necessary addition to present hospice organizations would be the incorporation of staff trained specifically to deal with the emotional and psychological needs of children from infancy to adolescence and staff with experience in working with families of terminally ill children. Such additions would not pose any major problems. If hospice care for children were to be extended to inpatient facilities, modifications would be necessary to create a suitable environment for the children.

Maintenance of the family as a cohesive, supportive unit, provision for the relief of loneliness and separation anxiety, and symptom controls for the maximum comfort and alertness of the dying child are the key objectives for an inpatient or home care hospice program.

Appendix A

The Gift of David:
His Care and Death at Home
by Leah Loveday

(To the One Who Taught Us So Much Through David)

> *The leaf falls from the tree's arm,*
> *Doing loops and rolls in the autumn air,*
> *And as it tumbles to the ground it sends a*
> *Small breeze gently over the green grass.*
> *Not moving it,*
> *Not disturbing it,*
> *But quenching it,*
> *Cooling it.*
>
> —David Loveday

"What was it, Mom?" David whispered, still groggy from the surgery a few hours before. "It was a tumor, David." I whispered back, all I could say without tears. Too sleepy for more questions, David nodded.

Yesterday was Thanksgiving. David's hospital admission was scheduled for late afternoon to give us time for dinner. Exhausted from numerous tests and examinations over the previous weeks, with diagnoses as varied as abcessed liver, amoebas, etc., David did not feel up to socializing. So Grandma and Poppa brought over a little Thanksgiving feast with a chicken stuffed and sewed and baked to look like a turkey. None of us felt too cheery, and after a nap David reminded me to get ready for the hospital. After days of hearing David say of himself at the clinic, "David's so tired," "David doesn't want to be here," or "David's scared," his firmness as he said, "I don't think we should be late, Mom," surprised me.

David, as usual, refused a wheelchair and walked into the hospital unassisted. As a grown-up twelve-year-old, he answered most admission questions himself. Later that evening, Tom (David's father) and Doug (his identical twin brother) drove down from the town in which they live in northern Arizona. Douglas, whose sense of humor often saved us, clowned around, as David soberly commented to me, "Sometimes Doug embarrasses me!"

Tom, my former husband, and I were there early in the morning, with time for me to bathe David, who was quite cheerful, and for Tom to chat with the pediatric surgeons. We walked with David in his bed up to the operating room, and he let my hand go just as they wheeled him in. Then the long (actually two hours') wait, part of which time I spent in the chapel. I thought of all the people who'd sat there like me, waiting. Then I walked restlessly back to the crowded, dull waiting room where the pediatric surgeons motioned me out to the hallway.

As we stood in the hallway, they bluntly told me the news—cancer; a large tumor on the liver that had metastasized throughout David's chest and lungs. This news had to be repeated as Tom joined us a few moments later. In shock, I heard them say they'd sent samples to the lab to find out more about what variety of cancer it was. When I mentioned withholding the news from David, one of the surgeons said, very wisely, "No, he must be told the truth. He's a bright boy, and we'll be doing many unpleasant things to him. He'll need to know why!" Though I would have appreciated a seat while being told, and though I was too stunned to understand the tests he referred to, I always appreciated this doctor's compassion and empathy. Later, while gently talking to David, he mentioned his own son, who was David's age.

So, there we were, Tom and I, crying in each others arms. Actually, I'm not sure what we talked of, for I had a persistent sense of unreality that chilly November morning. "This can't be real" ran through both our minds. There was just time for a bit of crying and talk (though it seemed long), before getting ourselves ready to go back to the crowded pediatric ward to greet David.

We arrived just as he was being transferred to his bed, surrounded by tubes—an I.V. and one from his nose to stomach. He looked very pale. He greeted us, "Mom, Dad." Later that afternoon, while I was either in the busy hallway sobbing or at home getting ready to spend the night at the hospital, David asked Tom, "Was it cancer?" Tom nodded. David lay still, and for the next few days just looked at us with those large sad eyes.

Friends rallied round. Some answered the phone for me and spread the news, sparing me the heartbreaking repetition. Many brought food and thermoses of tea while Tom or I stayed at the hospital. Others kindly drove me to the hospital, as my body often trembled for a number of days and I suffered from dizziness [as noted in earlier chapters under somatic symptoms of grief]. I tried to pray, but all I could do was cry.

The evening after surgery, David motioned me close and asked to pray. Very intensely, he prayed to God to heal his liver "in the most gentlest way." "Even if it means more surgery," he assured me. "And we won't forget," he promised God. My prayers too, for the first day, were for David's life; but soon they were for his pain to be minimal. It was very hard to stay in the present as I kept thinking, "I don't want to be here, I don't want this to be happening." Late that night, as David's stomach tube was adjusted, it was as if I felt it in my stomach too. I felt faint. Kind nurses thought I had the flu and went out of their way to get me a cup of tea.

The next few days were full. Dr. Hutter, a pediatric hematologist-oncologist, met with us and explained the results of tests so far and described tests David would have. Each bit of news was graver. Not only had they found cancer, but a type resistant to radiation and chemotherapy. Dr. Hutter said hopefully, "There is still much we can do for David." In his visits with David, Dr. Hutter always gave us the feeling that he had time to answer any questions we needed to ask, and he invariably asked David if he had any. David did. "Why didn't they take the tumor out?" "Because," Dr. Hutter explained, "it was connected with tissues you need," and spread his fingers to show David how it was connected. "What did it look like? I imagine it to look large and chocolate brown," David asked. Dr. Hutter nodded. Dr. Hutter established the ideal patient-doctor relationship [as described in Chapter 2]; David was satisfied with his answers and had full confidence in him.

David later asked me, "Do you think doctors are sorry to tell a boy he has cancer?" When I described one surgeon as having tears in his eyes and the love and concern I felt from all of them, he nodded, comforted.

Adding to my grief, though, was David's anger and criticism of me as I helped him sit or stand. Fortunately, the social worker met with us once in the hospital and explained that it was safe for him to vent his anger on me. That helped me take it less personally and realize how temporary it was. David's anger only seemed directed to me when he was particularly frustrated with illness or during hospitalization.

He was in great pain, for the incision had covered his abdomen and part of his chest, but using his will and determination, David stood up and walked. It was touching to see him, with great effort, sit in a chair to watch football on television.

A boy across from David was the same age and was hospitalized for having injured his liver during a bicycle accident. Ruefully, we remembered how we'd thought David's pain had come from a fall on his bicycle handles. David and the other boys chatted a bit and sent each other packs of gum or other little presents. A teenager across from David was covered with scratches, casts, bandages, and bruises from a mountain fall while hiking. David whispered to me, "Wish that was what I had!"

❊　❊　❊

You have to leave the surface of the ocean to reach the depths.
You have to leave the lowlands to reach the mountain peaks.
—Swami Amar Jyoti, *Retreat into Eternity*, p. 60

When ready to go home, David decided to go to Grandma and Poppa's house for "a little vacation." Depressed, he often lay on the couch with his back to us. He called to me and opened his arms wide, and as I hugged him his first evening out of the hospital, he said sadly, sounding so old, "I call for my Mom and it doesn't help." The twinkly-eyed boy with his cheery "Hi, Momeee!" was gone.

As his spirits lifted and the incision healed, he began to do some art work. Using some clay Grandma has for her pottery, he sculpted a tiny (scarcely three-inch) strange-looking devil with a big grin. He refused to comment. Always artistic, he drew many cards for us, usually decorated with objects he saw around him. His drawing had begun to change though, for he no longer drew airplanes, animals, and fish as he used to. One day, with earnest concentration, he drew a fantasy spacescape in soft pastel tones with colored pencils; there were small bubblelike planets in the upper right corner and two abstract oblong shapes, perhaps guides for a golden pod from the lower left corner. The golden pod had an inner pod surrounded by green plantlike spikes. Inside the central portion of the pod, like an embryo, was a lovely sprouting seed. It was an unusual drawing for a twelve-year-old boy and was unusual for David. Again he had no comment.

We had many visitors and one, a lovely lady who we knew had cancer, came and talked to David. "Cancer is just another name," she said. "I think of myself as having an illness: It's an illness of confused cells that aren't getting clear messages from the brain." She encouraged David to do what he could to get well. He appreciated her explanation and called her "a messenger." Later, when we read Madeleine L'Engle's *A Wind in the Door*, he said, "Charles is a boy like me, with confused cells."

We began work with Dr. Rose Tennant on healing imagery, autogenics (deep relaxation), and a kind of meditation. With such guided practice in mind control and autosuggestion, David often experienced remarkable results. After his first session, his shirt was soaked with sweat. Dr. Tennant explained to me that he'd had a powerful radiation treatment in which he'd imagined the sun's rays. He clearly had more energy and less pain after a session too. At the end of his first visit, Dr. Tennant asked, "What happened a year ago?" "Uncle Richard died," David answered, his eyes full of tears. That evening he cried and cried in my arms and kept saying, "I didn't know," for he hadn't shown any grief the year before. Then, tired, "Well, that's enough for tonight but we'll do more to-morrow. I want Dad and Doug to know this." He called them on the phone and explained on their next weekend visit all that he was learning about his feelings, suppression, and disease. We also lis-tened to a Simonton tape* Dr. Tennant loaned us and felt greatly encouraged as the patient described his healing through guided im-agery. With Dr. Tennant David quickly cleared up his short past and said to me happily, "I forgive everybody for everything." Dr. Tennant was impressed and expressed her admiration many times.

Dr. Hutter encouraged David's work with Dr. Tennant and often said, "I'm pleased with how well you're doing with pain," al-though, of course, he also prescribed medication.

Dr. Hutter also helped us by holding a meeting a few weeks after David's surgery. Tom drove down with his girl friend, Doug, and Grandma V. All interested friends were welcome, and Grandma and Poppa. David was invited too, but decided not to come. Ten-sion filled me just walking through the hospital lobby, and I was not looking forward to the meeting. At the conference room door there were many loving friends (who had notified each other)—about twenty-five people. Many had taken time from work to attend, and the love and support coming through was immeasurably comfort-ing. Dr. Hutter explained David's cancer, described treatment available and the sort of chemotherapy he could offer. Then, with his usual calm, he opened the discussion for questions. Some of the men with scientific backgrounds asked questions that hadn't oc-cured to me, and from the answers we realized that no one with pri-mary cancer of the liver had ever been cured by chemotherapy. At

*Dr. O. Carl Simonton is an oncologist with a center in Texas. His patients use visualization to heal themselves.

the most it *might* shrink the tumor a bit, but with great cost to the patient—a hospital stay, an incision for insertion of a catheter into the hepatic artery, nausea, loss of hair, etc., and very little hope of success. It didn't sound very promising. Dr. Hutter also said something very important to us—that he would continue as David's doctor no matter what our decision. Gently he answered Poppa, who asked angrily why the cancer hadn't been found earlier. Primary liver cancer is extremely rare in children, so rare that each major cancer center sees scarcely one case a year. Understandably, the doctors hadn't looked for it. Also, by the time David felt the pain in his right shoulder, the tumor was already quite large. Many asked other questions, but the benefits of this meeting were not only in the answers given, but in the unity it brought us. Everyone understood the gravity of David's situation. Nearly everyone stuck with us and helped one way or another during the new few months. This meeting helped make David's care a community effort. Doug said later, "I'm not a vibe detector, but there were good vibes there." We left the conference room with lighter hearts, our burdens shared.

A friend left the meeting a bit early and stopped at my house and heard "a sweet little voice singing." David was singing all alone. He told me he often made up songs but refused to sing if anyone was around. He made up little cancer jokes too (not all of which he repeated to me). For instance, while reading a silly story together in which an animal ate all sorts of strange things David said, "Oh, oh, he better watch out, he might get cancer." Or while I read the ingredients on a pack of sugarless gum, "It's all right, Mom, I can have it. I don't have to worry about getting cancer."

My appreciation for David grew more and more as he taught me with his wise innocence. After hearing me pray, he said simply, "Does it have to have all that fancy stuff to work? I just pray until I feel satisfied inside." He felt my evasions of "maybe" or "I guess so" were dishonest, and he urged me to tell the truth.

Our weekly clinic visits at the University of Arizona Hospital continued, with ultrasound examinations every other week.

David's letters to Tom and Doug are like a diary of our December activities.

> I wish you were here Doug. I miss you, but I'm not bored. It seems like every day I have plenty of things to do like seeing the accupuncturist, the three times a day relaxation tape, seeing Dr. Hutter or Cample. I'm really busy sometimes. For favorite pastimes I listen to Mark Twain storie tapes from the library, or mom reads to me from fiction books. I can't wait till Christmas, Aunt Gwen and Uncle Jim mailed some Christmas presents for me and you and mom won't let me open them till Christmas. Love David.

Or to Tom:

> I miss you and want to see you. Today I had another ultra sound. I can't wait to see you. Also I can't wait for Christmas. Yesterday I got a hair cut and I look exactly like Douglas. I'm having a very nice time. Yesterday I had a accupuncture treatment and felt real good, full of energy and this good feeling has lasted throughout today. It's just one more reason I feel I should try this before Kemotherapy. I'm eating well and feeling good. Love David Merry Christmas.

He also wrote about "keeping souvenirs of my experiences with doctors." And in a letter to Tom's girl friend:

> I miss you, and enjoy your warm feelings. I'm glad your coming and can't wait to see you . . . . I feel real good and more energy than normal, today and yesterday. It rained today. I like this whether a lot, it's more Christmas whether than yesterday. Yesterday it was hot. I'm living in a real cute house, with a cute little Christmas tree that's only about 3 feet tall. Love, David Merry Christmas.

He was eager to give presents and pushed himself to go shopping. Though we chose quieter stores, he was still very fatigued. Eager to have each present look nice, he spent more on bows, matching paper, and fancy cards than on gifts and took considerable care to wrap each one. All of his cards and letters were lavishly decorated.

He sent Christmas cards to everyone, including each doctor, as well as thank-you notes to all who sent gifts. David said, "I understand how important letters are now." Mostly he printed, in tinier and tinier letters as his disease progressed.

Tom, Doug, and Grandma V drove down for David's long-awaited Christmas. Grandma V brought a turkey, and along with Poppa and Grandma we had a large family dinner for the first time in many years. Doug was good-natured about all the presents David received and helped him unwrap them. Together they chuckled over amusing gifts, though David was too tired for most. Everyone seemed so jolly, except that Tom began to cry as we listened to Lionel Barrymore in *A Christmas Carol* on the radio. The sky was gray and the day chilly, which matched my mood. I was too sad at Christmas to enjoy the family meal and could not pretend holiday cheer.

David felt more stress too. Whether it was the post-Christmas mood, or the presence of so many in our tiny house, or just the course of the disease, the pain grew worse. We were up more frequently at night and it was harder for him to relax. My heart sore after a wakeful night, I called to speak to a colleague of Dr. Hutter, who was out of town. The cold words "Well, as this thing gets bigger it's bound to cause more pain" brought no comfort. David was now taking a stronger form of codeine and valium.

Doug, even with his sense of humor, grew quieter also. He handled all the attention given David well, though he once opened the door to visitors saying, "Hi, you got any presents? I'm the one who's sick." He developed a sore throat for several days during Christmas vacation and wanted to stay in bed, have hot tea and love and sympathy like David—which we gave. Tom was very understanding and helped me see how hard it was for Doug, who said, "I wish I were on fast forward or rewind." David changed. He grew less interested in boyish things. This was hard for Douglas. He began to feel cut off from David. Douglas had a frightening dream in which David wouldn't talk to him.

We all had vivid or frightening dreams that December. David

dreamed that a dangerous woman, who caused accidents, left notes that read, "Berries are beautiful, but they drop off." My dreams were of losing a child, or sick children over and over.

Christmas was over. Relatives were gone. The new year had begun. David was weak, tired, and depressed, but there was some relief too as he could relax more deeply in our quiet house.

✻　✻　✻

Actually, "troubles" have a two-fold purpose in the Divine play. They are the fruits of past misdeeds, and at the same time, they purify the dross and open inner potentialities of strength and wisdom.
—Swami Amar Jyoti, *Retreat into Eternity*, p. 101

Laboriously changing from pajamas and slippers to "regular" clothes, with socks pulled up just right and tennis shoes (for David insisted on being properly dressed), to go to the pediatric oncology clinic, David commented on his appearance. "I'm so skinny now. Will people think I look different?" Since early childhood David expressed a desire to "be normal," and he'd been fearful of being different. He explained the difference between his "real self" and his "normal" social self. David said, "God helps people to be their 'real' selves. My 'real' self's coming out with this illness. I used to have one for the crowd." The superfluous personality, the "one for the crowd," fell away completely during his illness.

Concerned for us, David asked about finances. "I don't want to be the boy who takes all the bacon." The income I had from disability payments was low, and Tom's insurance wouldn't cover this, so David was greatly reassured when Crippled Children's Services covered surgery, hospitalization, and visits to Dr. Hutter. He felt as grateful as I did that God provided everything we needed. Even a couch with a hide-a-bed showed up at our house after David's surgery. We both relaxed, trusting that our needs would be met, and they were.

When sent a little money by relatives, David would lie quietly and think of presents to give: an apple pie for Poppa, gift certificates to his favorite restaurant for friends who helped us. He'd give gift certificates himself. He enjoyed giving so much that we bought more certificates when his money ran out. He saved special candy to give Dr. Hutter and the graduate student nurse. He shared ice cream with any child who came to visit. David gave his small savings to Douglas "to go fishing in Michigan 'cause I don't need anything." We never said it, but in a way he was making out his will.

Flexibility was one of the lessons of David's illness and our lives continued to change as his pain increased and mobility decreased. Spending more time in bed by January, David insisted on sleeping on the hide-a-bed in the living room. The bedroom was "a hide-away-room," he said. So friends helped me rearrange furniture. Such loud noises as the vacuum cleaner or a screen door slamming were too disturbing. "The vibrations hurt my stomach," David said. A stopper was put on the screen door and the vacuum retired. The telephone was also moved to what had been David's bedroom. Even his little singing canary, whom he named "Sounder," was often too much and was moved away from his bed. Grandma and Poppa bought soft running suits as substitutes for jeans, so David was more comfortable and still properly dressed for outings, as he preferred.

Clearly, too, he wanted as much of my time and attention as possible [see Chapter 6]. One of the doctors had suggested a puppy for David. Though it would have been fun, he logically explained to Tom on the phone, "We decided against it because it would take up a lot of Mom's time, and I want all her time now. I don't even like it when she spends too long at the clothesline." As one friend urged, it was time for me to accept help with such chores as laundry.

At about this time he said very simply that he wasn't afraid of dying and "wouldn't mind it, but you'd mind it," as if he were living for me. He was right; it was so hard to let go, to imagine life without him. I did mind it. His acceptance speeded my acceptance. I wanted David to feel free to speak. A woman I knew, a nurse at a hospice, stopped by one day and I expressed these concerns to her. She chatted with David and encouraged him to take his pain pills before he felt pain, to continue on a regular schedule. She explained the reasons for this. Then she asked if he thought about death. He did but was afraid "Mom will be sad." "Mommy will be sad," she said, "but she can take it." I assured him I could.

Grandma, who was present, was shocked to hear us talking about death, for to her it meant giving up. But after David and I passed along Elisabeth Kübler-Ross's *Live until We Say Goodbye*, she and Poppa began to accept also.

We had had philosophical talks since David's early childhood, but now our discussions turned more frequently to death. Sometimes I described my belief that there was really no such thing as death, that the spirit or soul, the part that was of God, survived. David's face would just glow and he'd say with pleasure, "you understand." The peace that surrounded us was so great it was as if we could feel God protecting us. (Neighbors, friends, and Kathi, the graduate student nurse, all commented on it.) I would say to David as he lay in bed, "We are so fortunate, David," and he'd nod his agreement.

He dictated the poem that appears at the beginning of this appendix, after much pleading from me. He made up many poems in his head, but hesitated to tell them for fear of "showing off." After telling me this poem, he said his guardian angel's name was "Leaves, with both meanings."

Late one January night David complained of difficulty with breathing. After several phone calls I took him to the emergency room, with the help of my friend Carmella (which meant I didn't have to leave him alone while parking the car). X-rays revealed that the tumor was pushing up against his lungs, so there was less space for him to use. Phone calls to Dr. Hutter and discussion with David led to David's decision to stay at the hospital where he could get oxygen. Examinations and interviews lasted late, and it was 3:00 A.M. before we went to sleep. Fortunately, David's room was large and had no other occupant for several nights. I pushed a few chairs together and stayed with him. I woke in the morning to see a nurse bending over him, gently stroking his face saying, "He has the face of an angel."

Lucy, one of David's favorite grown-ups, took him around one day in a wheelchair, while I left the hospital for a while. They visited the "babies," for David was concerned about children who were ill. They met a father with a little girl called "Karma." When told of David's cancer, the father encouraged him with "So, you're one of the lucky ones who doesn't have to wait until he's old to be good enough to leave. You're good enough now." David felt more cheerful after hearing this "messenger" and said "he understood." When we went back that evening the man and his daughter were gone.

Friends brought food, a change of clothes, love, and support. There was anger and depression too [see Chapter 5], for each hospitalization is a reminder. Even though we talked of death, David and I had been pretending that he was just ill and would get better.

Kathi, the graduate student nurse who became our daily link with Dr. Hutter, arranged for oxygen at home and, through the M.S. Sick Room Loan Chest, for the loan of a hospital bed and a wheelchair. She even arranged for the pick up by some of our ever-kind friends.

Home again, David decided to stay enrolled in a homebound teaching program, but he never felt able to see the teacher again. He decided against further acupuncture and wanted to discontinue several other remedies (such as the grape poultice, which he felt had helped him). Tom continued to research, but found no successful treatments for David's case. The imagery and relaxation continued and helped control the pain.

For about a week after the hospitalization, David pushed his strength to do all the things he enjoyed. Treated by our friends, and Grandma and Poppa, we went out for lunch, or dinner, or to movies. The wheelchair couldn't be used on the gravel driveway or our brick walk and it was torturous for him to climb in and out of the car. A birthday party he looked forward to, which was for grown-ups and children of all ages, proved exhausting. Outings, even to the clinic, were no longer possible. So David gave them up without a comment. As a friend remarked later, "He did whatever he could until he couldn't do it anymore. Then he'd give it up without looking back. He might be a little disgusted, but he'd give it up."

⚜   ⚜   ⚜

You have to be bold in mind to not be threatened by the frankness of Truth. There is no darkness if you face the sun.
—Swami Amar Jyoti, *Retreat into Eternity*, p. 106

Bedbound now, except for walking to the bathroom, David could still sit up to eat from a hospital tray. His abdomen, distended and swollen, made even loose pajamas uncomfortable. David said he wanted "little nightgowns," about to his knees, so he chose the colors and we ordered large men's T-shirts from a catalog. Tom and my friends' husbands contributed their old shirts too. With oxygen tanks, hospital bed, hospital tray, and our small television propped up so he could reach it, the living room was full. It was cheerful, though, as David picked out pictures of animals for the walls and told me where to hang the crystals and decals he enjoyed. He was surrounded by flowers from friendly gardens and valentines, for it was February. Little "Sounder" kept singing, and we had tapes of gentle music. From his bed he could see hummingbirds at the feeder on the tree outside the window. Preferring home [see Chapter 6], he once told the social worker, "If it weren't for my mom and her friends I'd be in some hospital." Quiet, no longer able to write and draw, David said he wasn't bored "because I have a lot to think about."

With growing acceptance, his depression was gone. No tears, no self-pity, just occasional irritability because "this disease is so frustrating." He apologized for his "grumpiness" and prayed to God for help. Grumpiness was certainly forgivable with his physical stress: bouts of diarrhea, vomiting, constant pain, weakness, painful urination, legs that felt like a "a thousand ants were biting," headaches, backaches, and nosebleeds.

Yet with all this, David had no complaints and even was happy! His frequent message to us was, "I am happy and I will be happy." He wanted everyone he loved to "understand the way I want them to" before he died. He wanted to teach others, especially Tom and Doug (whom he said "might not be ready for another year"). He had so much to teach me with his rare words, and he commented on my "understanding." He said once, "We really are one; when you relax, I relax too." One midnight, after receiving his Demerol, he said, "I'm comfortable. Don't fill your mind with thoughts and trouble yourself." Later the next day he reminded me, "You think too much."

One evening, as I helped him walk to the bathroom, he compared himself to how he used to be, how he'd been able to run and be active and had never thought he'd be "crippled." "But I'm not complaining and wouldn't change anything. I'm not sorry I've got cancer; I've learned so much. Aren't you glad to have asthma?" I couldn't answer him. His voice was so sincere and full of gratitude, and I'd never reached his maturity.

He told Tom that he was happy, not sad, he'd had cancer because he learned a lot. He wanted Tom to understand and accept because "there's no reason to be sad or angry."

When asked once if he had anything he wanted to say to anyone, he repeated, "I want everyone to understand not to be sad." David was calm, at peace, unafraid, and generally in control. His prayer for faith had been generously answered. He said he'd go to God "like a mom or dad, not as a leader," and that I should go to God in that way too.

Douglas had a good talk with David one night. They talked about death and David was very practical and matter-of-fact. He paraphrased a taped discourse of Swami Amar Jyoti we'd listened to: "When you accept the entrance you have to accept the exit." Douglas felt better and told David he was glad to hear he wasn't afraid and that "the body was to express the soul." When David nodded, Doug exclaimed of himself, "I didn't know I knew that." The discussion was a relief, for it had been a lonely evening for Doug. He'd borrowed games from our next-door neighbors and then realized, in great disappointment, that there was no one to play with him.

Around 1:30 one morning David woke up and joyfully told me he'd had a wonderful dream and knew everything would be all right.

> I was in an enclosed area like in front of Dr. Tennant's office with grass and trees and a cement sidewalk. Doug and I are running around and playing and I feel so happy to be well and running. Mom is sitting down talking to a tall dark, suntanned man with beard and mustache. The man says to me, "Be careful not to run into the lower limbs." I said (sarcastically), "Yes, I will, I'll run right into them." Then I was sorry I said that and apologized to the man in my mind. The man is helping me (maybe my guardian angel). Dr. Tennant is standing near one of the trees with tears in her eyes because she is so happy to see me well and running. I am so glad I feel like crying too.

Still glowing from his dream, David said he might leave for a while and get some "light nourishment."

We were up most nights from 12:00 to 1:30 or 2:00, and usually David had a snack and I read to him. They were cozy times, and as Grandma and friends took over laundry, shopping, and outside errands, I was able to rest more. We read the psalms a few mornings, as the sun came up, but more frequently books like *My Side of the Mountain, The Secret Garden, The Little Prince,* those by Madeleine L'Engle, Richard Bach, George MacDonald, and some Robert Louis Stevenson. Those about nature reminded David of how much he loved the mountains and lakes, and of how he missed that part of his life.

Wasting and pale, with more coughing and diminishing appetite, David was less and less inclined to talk. I treasured his whispered late-night words, the closeness, and his rare hug, kiss, or "Mommy, I love you so much!"

We began to play a fantasy game at night. I told him about pretend fishing trips with Douglas and Tom. David added details such as: bringing oxygen and wheelchair along in case he got tired, grateful for being well enough to go, going on a long walk alone with Mom ("we always had our talks"). In one pretend camping trip we were rained out and had to take a motel room. He added, "Douglas and David go next door to the flower shop, when their mom doesn't know, and buy her some flowers." On a pretend fishing trip I added a detail of canteens of water for him and Douglas, and he interrupted impatiently, "Mom, we've got our hands full with tackle and fishing rods, we can't carry canteens; we'll come back for water."

One night, in distress, he told me he heard bells or cricket chirps very loudly and persistently. He thought I might be playing a trick on him in the other room. The sounds were there with or without Demerol, so we didn't think that was the reason. I read him a section of Swami Amar Jyoti's *Spirit of Himalaya*, on Nada Yoga, the yoga of sound, which describes cricket chirps and bells among other sounds. I told him that even though I did not hear, or see, all the things he heard and saw it didn't make it less real or less normal. He seemed to relax after that, and even though the sounds continued, he was not distressed by them.

✄　✄　✄

There is no greater hell than doubts.
Faith is the temple of virtues.
—Swami Amar Jyoti, Retreat into Eternity, p. 94

Calm amidst greater physical stress (numbness on his left side, a lump near his collarbone getting bigger), he still wanted to comfort me. "Don't try to read my mind and upset yourself," he said with a smile as he held my hand. Or late at night, looking at me with lustrous eyes, "I can feel your love," giving my hand a squeeze. He could now tolerate my sadness, and once as I was about to leave the room, "It's all right; you can cry in here," then patted me gently as I wept.

He really emanated a sense of peace as he said, "I hope you feel as good as I do."

David fell twice one March day, which scared us both. Usually I waited for him outside the bathroom door until he was ready to go back to bed. Legs wasting and abdomen increasingly heavy, it was hard to balance and he fell, cutting his mouth. We agreed that the next time he was to ring for me before getting up by himself. But he wanted to try by himself again, and he fell, bruising his leg. He cried for just a minute after the second fall, saying, "I'm so stupid." He was quiet and thoughtful afterward. We rented a porta-commode, which was easier.

My distress was increasing also; less sleep, more work, and grief led to increased asthma. Yet we were blessed abundantly with kind friends, David's calm and peace, and unusual care from doctors (Drs. Hutter and Tennant made house calls every week). Kathi, who brought us supplies from the hospital and picked up David's prescriptions, said our environment was "utopia for this kind of situation" and described witnessing screaming kids with I.V.s of morphine and desperate parents. God's care and support were all around, yet I made myself miserable by thinking David might have been saved had I been more devoted. I was ashamed and felt guilty about my anger and rebellion and underestimated God's great love. In spite of my doubts, however, God continued to bless us.

Now and then David still remarked on death. "I have something to say," he said, taking off the oxygen mask for a moment to speak. "When someone dies it's that person's will. Like Uncle Richard. He wanted to die." Or, referring to Bach's *Illusions*, "Even Donald Shimoda got shot. Everybody has to die. So, it's no surprise." He nodded when I asked if this comforted him. Yet sometimes he would speak of living, and of doing the things he enjoyed again. "There's so much I still want to do!"

We'd had record-breaking rains and winds that year, with floods in Phoenix. In spite of the cold, David complained of heat and needed a fan from February on. His abdomen was hot, yet his feet and arms were cold. As he could no longer bend at the waist, it became impossible for him to sit up, which made it difficult for me to change his shirt without help. Shirts bunched up behind him, so we abandoned them. Socks with toes cut off became cozy sleeves, and socks and towels were his lower garments.

His face was less and less a child's as it became thinner. Pale, with finer hair, arms and legs skeletal, he still was beautiful. Perhaps his body was no longer attractive, but his large eyes reflected his spirit, for which the only word was *beautiful*. Most women commented on David's beauty: Dr. Tennant, Kathi, Grandma, and all my female friends. To me, with his sleeve-socks and arms crossed over his chest, he was till lovable, still David. When praised for courage, or for anything else, David would protest, "It's not me; it's just my situation."

Kathi met my need for "limiting uncertainty" [see Chapter 5] and said the most likely ends were hemorrhage, or gradual suffocation, which would be more peaceful. When I repeated David's remark "I could have gone crazy with this, but I like this way better," I was surprised at her reaction. "How could he have known?" she exclaimed. I didn't know either so she explained that liver failure often leads to craziness as toxins are released in the blood stream. By God's grace David's liver did not fail and he was able to eat surprisingly well. "His stomach must be the size of a quarter," Kathi said with wonder.

Eating was still a pleasure for David, and a comfort to us. Knowing that people often wanted to be able to do something useful, he sent people on errands to bring him tempting foods. After a friend and I had lifted him clumsily one day, he lay still and pale with pain. My heart was sore, then lightened considerably as David opened his eyes and whispered, "Arby's" to Grandma. Naturally, she was delighted to go. He kept Tom busy too, and all the ladies who baked enjoyed filling his food requests. As he once said guilelessly to Doug, "People bring me all my favorite foods. You want something? A banana split? You watch, I'll just ask." His diet had gone from natural foods after his surgery to a mother's horror. As Dr. Hutter explained, David's liver could best assimilate sugar now, and he also had a need for calories. As Easter approached, it seemed as if he lived on ice cream, cake and cookies, cereal, fruit, kefir, and protein drinks. Once, protesting the candy and goodies, I said, "David, it's awfully hard for me to feed you a sugar diet." He just looked at me and grinned, a huge grin on his emaciated face. I laughed and stopped protesting.

Though most visitors were adults, he had some contact with children. His desire to meet other boys his age with cancer, and Kathi's search, led to a fellow with leukemia in remission. The visit (while David was still walking) had gone well, but was exhausting. Children near his age wanted his social attention and conversation, which became too tiring. Those of my friends with little children sometimes stopped by, to David's amusement. Little ones just accepted David as he was and didn't ask anything of him. David expressed a lot of affection and concern for young children and was quite fond of the toddler and baby next door. He was still a part of the community of neighbors, grandparents, and friends [see Chapter 6]. As he became bedridden, the only two of his age he felt comfortable with were Douglas and Ruth's daughter, Anna.

When Ruth visited during the day, Anna accompanied her and understood the quiet David needed. They never spoke, but Ruth and I sensed their communication as Anna silently sat near his bed. David remarked once after Anna's visit, "Grown-ups make it hard for a boy and girl to be friends. I like Anna. She's a nice simple person and doesn't ask me questions." Around Easter, Ruth and Anna came one afternoon, for David was comfortable with them, and Tom and I could take some needed rest. David had been up often at night and lay very still, eyes rolling involuntarily, so that people sometimes wondered if he were conscious or not. As Ruth told me later, "David lay there with his eyes rolling, then opened them, focused clearly on Anna, and gave her a big grin."

❧ ❧ ❧

Certain trials and challenges beset you. But the more you accept the tests, the more powerful you become. Truth does bestow strength.
—Swami Amar Jyoti, *Retreat into Eternity*, p. 83

It was Easter week, and Tom and Doug came down to spend their vacation with us. Though friends had helped out at night, with Tom there, camped out in the living room, it meant some real sleep at night for me. David was most comfortable with Tom or me, and shy about some things in front of others, no matter how much he loved them. For some time he'd wanted only Tom there if I were going out and vice versa. For Tom it was an opportunity to participate more fully in David's care. David's silence, and the physical separation, had led Tom to feel that David had already left. Being there over a longer period, and hearing David's whispered comments, helped Tom to feel that David was still very much with us.

It meant time for me with Douglas also. Doug, after his initial grief over David's cancer ("He's my twin," he'd protested, "he can't die!"), had gotten involved with school and friends and was more reluctant to come down. We'd compromised, but sometimes I did insist he come. I felt some resentment, not understanding a child's manner of handling grief [see Chapter 3]. My wise friend Carmella advised compassion, and hugging Doug I felt his great sorrow. Doug and I even went out to breakfast one morning, and as he chatted about the bowling team and his friends it seemed another world to me. He and David had some nice moments together too. It was good to see them watch the "Muppets" together on television as they used to do. I left the room once as Doug held David's hand, but caught the words "We'll be close no matter what happens." Doug told me later about one of the nights he spent at our house when he got up and held David's hand and said, "I love you." David had said "I love you" to him also.

Easter came for David. One afternoon he shook violently with a convulsion. I held his shoulders gently and prayed that his end be a more peaceful time. I called for Tom, who'd just come in, and he phoned our emergency numbers, reaching Fran, the social worker. The violence and duration of the convulsion, and David's difficulty asking for Demerol afterward, made us fear he'd had a stroke. I prayed that his mind and speech be clear. We were blessed, for by 5:00 A.M. he asked for ginger ale clearly. The following night Tom called me into the room as David complained that his feet hurt. Taking his socks off we saw that they were even more swollen than usual, pink and hot, making the toe nails look shiny. Tom guessed it might be gout, as I went through our emergency numbers and talked to Kathi. With her help we adjusted David's pain medication so that he could sleep. Dr. Hutter, during the visit the next day, felt Tom might be right and David had another large pill to swallow, along with the diuretics. The skin on his feet peeled as if sunburned.

Toward the end of that week David spat out a broken tooth as he chewed a jelly bean. I was alarmed, fearing his bones were weakening, but David was unimpressed. "I don't care," he said, and just felt it was a loose tooth for which the "tooth fairy" should leave money. He was amazing, unexcited by all these bodily changes, calm, unafraid, with no self-pity. He seemed detached from his body and even said he was bored one day.

Toward the end of that stressful week, as Tom prepared to leave in a few days, my depression grew. So, leaving David in Tom's care one sunny afternoon, I visited Carmella and wept. I could no longer lift David and felt useless and helpless. I felt at the limit of physical and emotional strength and found myself with no time for anything other than David. I felt inadequate. "What does David want you to do?" she asked with compassion. "He wants me to sit and hold his hand," was my reply. My strength was limited and at its end; God's strength was infinite. Bowing my stubborn head at last, I left David and myself in God's care, where we had been all along.

Tom had not realized I was depressed, and recognizing that I needed help at night, we checked with Kathi on the cost and availability of a night nurse. We couldn't afford one, we found. Though we could have gotten funds for hospitalization, we couldn't for nursing care. Tom had only been able to come on alternate weekends because of the long drive and his work schedule. Rearranging his teaching, he agreed to come for Friday, Saturday, and Sunday nights. A few friends had volunteered on other nights, and soon other friends and my generous neighbors volunteered for the rest. My neighbor Jerry and his wife, Cris, were quite fond of David. Jerry had played football in college and still lifted weights, so he was in good shape to lift David gently. David loved them both and was satisfied to have Jerry fill in for Tom.

It was good David had two parents, for Tom also had many labor-saving ideas. He bought paper plates, handi-wipes, paper cups, take-out food at restaurants, and left me well supplied. Grandma and our friends sent over dinners, or came and cooked and helped with housework. There was nothing for me to do, but, as Tom said, "relax and enjoy it."

Peace became thicker as we relaxed and I held David's hand, sometimes for hours. The honeysuckle by the front door was blooming and the smells of spring pervaded. We both became quieter. There was some talk as David said one day, "I had a very unusual dream. I dreamt a baby and a blood clot came out of my mouth." I told him about a vivid series of comforting and wonderful dreams, which he said made him "feel comfortable." One was of the vastness of God, and in another I was told "that everyone has a role in God's play."

Miracles continued. One night David went through great pain as Kathi tried unsuccessfully to insert a catheter. He held my hand tightly as I prayed. We gave up, as David was finally able to urinate. David was able to urinate after that without a catheter and said gratefully, "I thank God every time I can pee." Dr. Tennant visited and gave David some imagery to work with, saying, "Though there are many things about your body you can't control, there are still some things you can." He never needed a catheter again and continued to live without tubes going in or out, which was a great blessing for a patient in his stage of cancer.

Signaling with his hand for me to come and sit, David asked for my story. I gave him an oral autobiography up to my teen years, which he liked. As do many children with their mothers, he felt he'd have liked me as a girl. He was especially sympathetic about the asthma and said he wished he'd been alive when I was young to help. Understanding and compassionate of my wheezing, he gave me advice on relaxing "during hard times." When asking me for something, he would add, "When you can," and smile sympathetically. Who was the adult and who the child? David was no longer a child to me, but a wise old friend.

✄   ✄   ✄

In death is always a new life.
—Swami Amar Jyoti,
Retreat into Eternity, p. 94

The Friday before David's death Dr. Hutter visited with two young doctors from the hospital, as he would be going out of town. He wanted us to know and feel comfortable with his substitutes. David was matter-of-fact about their visit. He was hungry and didn't want me to stop feeding him because the doctors were there.

The day was unusually hot for April, with temperatures up into the nineties, and David suffered. The purple splotches on his chest grew larger and his face was flushed with heat. The cooler pump wasn't working, so no water was running, making our house very hot. Until our landlord got home and could fix it, I sponged David off and put wet cloths on him. During all this misery he turned to me and said, "I feel good—inside."

Tom's car broke down on the freeway and he had to hitchhike into town late that afternoon, then make arrangements for towing the car.

David was peaceful that evening and asked for fruit salad, which was all he ate for the next few days, saying he was "through" with the ice cream.

Waking that morning around 3:00 A.M., as Tom slept, David said, "I see everything as a present and not a punishment. Everything could have been much worse. Daddy could have crashed."

The heat still bothered David, and he wanted the cooler on during the night and the curtains drawn during the day. Saturday morning we borrowed a large fan from Jerry and Cris. David began to look markedly different as his eyes sunk into the sockets. We kept a towel on his face, as his eyes were bothered by the drying wind of the fan. He was still flushed, and his tailbone was painful. It was difficult for him to get comfortable and he needed to be turned or adjusted every twenty minutes to an hour during the night.

Sunday was gray and cloudy, to David's great relief. He lay thinking quietly and came up with several ideas. The first he whispered to Tom: "A rubber swim raft." Tom went out with pleasure, bought one at the nearest drugstore, and inflated it on the portable oxygen tank. While Tom and Jerry held David, I quickly changed the sheets, putting the rubber raft underneath and his sheepskin on top. Then, as they gently lowered him, David sighed with pleasure, saying, "I love it." He also told Jerry he liked the weather, which had become rainy.

He whispered his other ideas to me. "Does Cris let the baby have sugar? Find out if she has teeth. Then buy a freezie for the baby and a popsickle for Leslie (the three-year-old) and get an orange one for me." He even had the finances worked out; he reminded me that he hadn't received any money for the tooth that fell out, or allowance recently. Reassuring him about the money, I arranged with Cris to get the popsickles.

His chest and face were so red I thought he might have an infection and called Kathi, who advised keeping a record of his temperature. To my surprise, I found that it was going down, something like: 97°, 96°, 95°, and 94° by Monday morning. Tom, in disbelief, tested the thermometer on himself, but his temperature was normal. Sunday night I prayed David's ordeal would be over soon and whispered to him, "You don't need to stay in your body and suffer anymore."

Tom needed to go back to work Monday morning and left just as Fran and the young doctors from the hospital arrived. The doctors found that David's potassium balance was off (from the diuretics) and he'd become dehydrated (hence the sunken eyes). We decreased some of his pills and increased foods with potassium in them (such as bananas and oranges—the fruit salad David requested). David was having more discomfort breathing and had trouble when the oxygen tank was changed. Raising his bed and increasing the oxygen flow seemed to help.

David wanted it quiet, as he had all weekend, and motioned to me to have visitors leave. We spent the day peacefully alone, quiet except for "Sounder." We both napped and held hands in silence that afternoon.

That evening Jerry came over to lift David. It was difficult to make him comfortable and Jerry took his time, even when Cris came to tell him a long-distance call waited at home. She'd also gotten the popsickles, but couldn't find an orange one. When I jokingly called Jerry "Superman" because of his size and strength, he nodded to David saying, "He's the Superman." Little Leslie had come too, and before they left David perked up, grinned at her, and said quite loudly, "Bye, Leslie."

Carmella came at about 10:00 P.M. and we both needed to get up each time during the night. David didn't call our names, as usual, but groaned. I urged, "If you're too tired to swallow the pills, I can crush them up." David replied in a firm whisper, "When I'm too tired to swallow, then we'll worry about it."

I really felt the change in him during the night, for we'd be talking, then suddenly he'd be gone. He'd needed the bed raised higher and was in more pain. My wheezing was fatiguing, but with Carmella's wise help, I was able to rest.

Tuesday morning there was further change in David. He had great pain urinating, but still was in control and wanted the urinal. Jerry came over and we had a hard time getting David comfortable. He too saw the change in David. When he'd gone, David said to me quite urgently, "Help me," then after a pause, "Go." I thought he meant urinate, but Douglas said he'd have said "pee" if he meant that.

Then David was out again (in a coma I learned later), but was groaning with his jaw clenched tight. Carmella and I found a syringe, ground his pills, and squirted them in when his jaw unclenched for a moment. I phoned the hospital and talked to Fran, who said she and the doctor would come as soon as possible. I thought David was in pain and asked the doctor to come prepared. Then I phoned Tom, and Grandma, so they'd be prepared for whatever happened, having no idea how long this might last.

Carmella had to leave, so I asked my good friend Constance to come. Then as I sat holding David's hand he seemed to relax. Fran, entering the room, answered my unspoken question right away with "It won't be long now." Fran and the doctor said David was in a coma and feeling no pain. I wanted to hold David so much, but was afraid of hurting him. It had been such a long time since I had been able to hold him. Both Fran and the doctor assured me it would not hurt David now and lifted him so I could climb into the bed and hold him in my arms. David seemed to relax more and surrender to what was happening as I held him. Constance was standing beside me, and I asked her to call Ruth.

After all the months of worry about David's death, worry about if I'd know, or if I'd be there, and here it was, in God's hands, unfolding perfectly. It grew very still. The wind died down, the oxygen was turned off, even "Sounder" was quiet. Tears flowed silently; we were a circle of love around David. Fran touched either me or David, the doctor touched me, and Constance and Ruth lightly touched either David or me. I lost track of anything happening in the room outside of David. I lost track of my resolution to pray and was totally absorbed. I lost track of time and was surprised later to find I'd held him for two hours.

Perhaps it's not accurate to say we (Constance, Ruth, and I) felt God's presence. It was more that we were within His presence, within His consciousness, within His great golden heart. The room was so peaceful; David's death was so perfect. All our desires were fulfilled. David and I had talked of him dying in my arms, which months ago he'd said "would be wonderful." I was so grateful to God for being there.

David's jaw and throat continued to work, which the doctor said was part of the process. David's chest was now purple, as the spots had continued to grow over the last hot days, and his heart kept beating, but all very peacefully. He uttered a last little sound, like a baby sound, which was his last breath. The hands moved up, as if toward my hand. He was gone. We all felt such calm and joy, a joy that was a surprise to all of us, unexpected. No more pain!

There was such joy in the room and peace that we even felt a kind of high. Grief in earnest didn't begin until later that night. David was free, a joyous spirit now.

To David with Love

I came to you
Thinking to give
And left, humbled
By what I had received

Your gifts were countless
The silent ones of
Dignity, Courage and Love
And the piercing ones
Of your voiced Wisdom and Truth

But the greatest of all
Was the privilege of sharing
In your unbounded Joy
As you became
            A Light-Being FREE!
Anonymous

Appendix B

Questions and Answers From Parents

This section grew out of discussions between a number of parents who've survived one or more of their children. The life span of these parents' children ranged from forty days to fourteen years; they died from cystic fibrosis, heart defects, heart attack, leukemia, and cancerous tumors. Though the ages of these children and the causes of their deaths varied, the parents all had the following concerns and questions in common.

DIAGNOSIS

This was the most difficult experience for most parents during the child's illness. They all asked: "Why? Why me? Why my child?"

Most of the parents realize that they may never have an answer. Perhaps for some of the parents the growth they and their children experienced, and the lives that were softened and touched by their children, are part of the answer.

Am I going crazy? Is this normal?

Parents frequently had these thoughts following the shock and pain of diagnosis. As they all felt numb and shocked and "crazy" for a while, this reaction seems to be "normal." All of them had a sense of being in a dream, and as one mother said, "I felt like I was watching Marcus Welby on TV." All of the parents wanted to be told of the diagnosis in some private area of the treatment center.

MEDICAL TREATMENT

Is my doctor doing all he can do for my child? Is he truthfully answering my questions? Is he explaining tests to me and my child?

Most of the parents had positive experiences with doctors and other medical personnel, and unfortunately, all of them had negative experiences as well. They felt anger and frustration when questions were ignored or were answered condescendingly. They saw their children treated as objects by some (though there were compassionate people as well). Overwhelmingly, parents asking these questions urge others to speak up and ask their doctors for information. Fathers tended to be more assertive and many mothers expressed regret over past timidity. Insist that explanations be given to your child as well, no matter how young. Most felt that their doctors did their best, did all they were capable of doing.

Parents urge others to accompany their child during treatments and tests and to insist upon this. The children were less frightened and at least had a hand to hold. Also, children cannot speak up for themselves and need their parents as advocates. More than one parent has had to insist on a new nurse after watching repeated unsuccessful attempts to insert an I.V. needle.

Parents also encourage others to follow their intuition, their gut feelings. One mother described her gut feeling that something was seriously wrong when her pediatrician dismissed her daughter's swollen eyes as an allergic reaction (the child died of acute leukemia a few months later). The same mother described trying to stop a nurse from an unnecessary sample-gathering procedure likely to cause hemorrhaging. The nurse insisted and indeed did start a dangerous hemorrhage. Parents can avoid much anger and frustration by finding a doctor who will take their concerns seriously. Parents (mothers especially) can avoid guilt and anguish later by following their intuition.

Did we fail to detect the early signs? What were the signs? What could we have done? How did the disease start? Would the outcome have been different if we'd known earlier?

Unfortunately, many of the early signs of some of the children's fatal diseases were similar to the symptoms of less serious illness. Intermittent fevers, stomach aches, and listlessness can look like a cold or the flu. Runny, puffy eyes and nose can look like an allergy. The list is endless. Again, parents urge others to follow their intuition. You know your child best and know when he or she is behaving differently. But even with all these observations, it is often difficult to catch the early signs of the disease. The doctors often had a difficult time with diagnosis; the parents with no medical experience are unlikely to detect early signs. The children often had diseases and treatments the parents were totally unfamiliar with. We just don't know how many of these diseases start, and as yet have no way to prevent them. The parents all loved their children and tried to provide the healthiest diet and environment they could for them before and after illness. What better preventive medicine could there be?

Perhaps events would have been different if detection were early enough, but as one mother remarked, "Not necessarily."

When the disease is hereditary there is a temptation for parents to blame each other, which adds to the pain of an already painful event. It took both parents to produce the child and the possibility of disease had to be carried by both. Parents with children stricken with a hereditary disease did not know they were carriers and in many cases had never heard of the disease before.

Can it happen again?

Young parents who wish to have more children are especially plagued by this question. When the disease is clearly hereditary the question is answered; but when the disease is not considered hereditary the possibility remains. One couple, whose child died of a heart defect, were assured the condition was not hereditary, only to have another child who also died from the same condition as a toddler. Many felt concern that the disease might show up later in healthy siblings. There are no answers, but there are statistics that indicate the likelihood of a disease being hereditary, or of showing up in other family members. Again, do not be shy—ask! If you are not satisfied with answers, ask the doctor to recommend some literature on the topic that you can read.

COPING

Is there another parent I can talk to who is going through this? Is there another child my child can relate to?

Most of the parents went through their child's illness and death isolated from others going through a similar experience. Many of them did not meet another bereaved parent until long after their child's death. All of them, and their dying children, would have liked knowing others. So many felt alone needlessly. If there is a Center for Attitudinal Healing in your area (see Appendix C), ask about parents' and children's groups. If not, ask the nurse or social worker for suggestions. If there is no Center for Attitudinal Healing near you, you can still apply for a phone/pen pal for you or your child.

What helped you cope?

Many parents were helped by religious faith and supportive friends. Some parents stressed knowledge about the disease as a coping factor. Reading about the condition, researching experimental methods, and learning about treatments available helped some parents cope. They felt this made the disease less foreign to them.

Most parents had to learn some treatment procedures to be followed at home (postural drainage for children with cystic fibrosis, for example). For some this was welcome, as it was something positive the parent could do for the child's well-being. Some saw this as a burden. Generally, though, the more the parents knew, and the more they could do, the less helpless they felt.

Both parent and child needed to be able to make choices whenever possible and to maintain some control over the situation. They felt less powerless, less helpless then. Even the youngest children needed options, needed to be able to make choices and to have their wishes respected.

How does a single parent cope?

It isn't easy, but it can be done. All of the single parents in this group were mothers, and all had financial problems requiring food stamps and other forms of state or government support. In some cases the child's father did participate in decision making and in care, usually on weekends. In several cases, the father was also present at the child's death. Even with the difficulties and stress of single parenthood, the mothers were able to care for their child at home, and with the cooperation of medical professionals and friends, some were able to have their child die at home also.

FAMILY AND FRIENDS
How can they help? Should parents accept help? What advice can parents give so that friends and relatives can help constructively?

There are so many ways to help. There is a role for everyone, and though all are not suited by temperament to give the child direct care, there are still many services the family needs. If you have a neighbor or friend who offers help, and you feel comfortable with that person, accept thankfully. Give choices. Perhaps you have a small list of needs, such as help with siblings while you must care for the sick child or be at the hospital, grocery shopping, errands, help with the house or meals, picking up prescriptions. If it is someone the child is comfortable with, you can accept help with the child's care and perhaps take a break yourself.

Friends and relatives can help best by tactfully accepting the situation. All of the parents received unnecessary though well-meaning advice. Sometimes people do have valid suggestions, but they must offer them tactfully, because the parent of a very sick child is emotionally vulnerable. Friends and family can also help by refraining from adding burdens; this is not the time to recite woes and complaints. The parents are preoccupied with their own concerns.

PREPARATION FOR DEATH
How will my child die? Is my child dying? Is my child afraid?

Every parent needed to know what was likely to happen at the end. None of them had had experience with a dying person before and they wanted to know what to expect. Some parents read about their child's disease and learned what to expect, but most wanted to ask questions. In almost every case the doctors were evasive in dealing with parents who had had unusually comfortable relationships with their doctors and had found them previously willing to answer questions. Most parents were answered more satisfactorily by social workers or nurses. Parents wanted to know as soon as possible when their child was dying. Any preparation they had about the changes likely to occur lessened their fear.

Those who were able to communicate openly with their children (called open awareness in earlier chapters) learned from them not to fear death and learned that they were not afraid. This was true with as young a child as a two-and-a-half-year-old, whose mother reported that the little girl comforted her older sister with "It'll be all right" and told her mother that she wanted "to go home." From songs the child sang, the mother understood that the child meant by "home" the dimension she would go to at death. Basically, this child, and David Loveday in "The Gift of David," said the same things. Those who were not able to discuss death with their children learned from remarks the children made to others that they were aware of dying and were not afraid.

DEATH
Will I use life-support systems? What will dying be like? Can parents be there while their child dies? Can they hold their child?

None of the parents decided to prolong their child's existence once it was apparent that the body could no longer function on its own. Older children requested that their parents not use life-support systems.

In some way each parent felt that they "let go," that they gave their child permission to die. They each had to find some acceptance inside in order to let their children go. This did not negate their grief, but allowed them to experience some measure of peace at the death.

They were all present at the deaths of their children, and though the breathing sounds of the dying were foreign to them, they were grateful to be there and felt peace and relief, especially if the child had been suffering. It was comforting to them to see their children without equipment, to see their faces uncluttered by oxygen or other apparatus. They all needed and wanted some quiet time alone with their child's body. For some it was the first opportunity in a long while to hold their child.

When death occurred at home, the parents had no difficulty getting time alone with their child; but when death occurred in the hospital, sometimes the parents were forced to insist on this. One couple watched the violent attempts to revive their ten-month-old from a heart attack and had to insist on remaining in the room, although nurses suggested they wait in the lobby. Then the father requested that he and his wife have time alone with their baby. The mother felt peace holding her baby after his long ordeal. Both parents are thankful they had this quiet time together with their son, whom they described as looking as if he were asleep.

For most parents, this quiet time alone with their child was a peaceful interlude in the midst of the turmoil before and after their child's death. Some of them would have liked more time with the child's body and later regretted not having asked for it.

Also, many parents do not know that they are not required to have an autopsy performed on the child's body. Part of a hospital's accreditation is based on the number of autopsies performed, so doctors ask, but parents do not have to consent.

Also, if the funeral home has a refrigeration room, parents are not compelled by law to have the body embalmed (though there may be variations from state to state). These are things parents are not told unless they ask.

GRIEF

Will the grieving parent ever be happy again? Can the family ever have good times again? What was the meaning of the child's life? Will grief ever go away?

All the parents went through deep grief after their child's death. The years pass, and most of these people are able to have good times with their families again. Sometimes they feel a lightness of heart they would have thought impossible after their child's death.

Yet all of them find that sorrow does remain, even after years. Sometimes it comes so unpredictably; they enter a situation feeling well able to handle it and find themselves sobbing again. The only suggestion is for parents to be patient with themselves. Do not tell yourself, "I should be over it by now." There are no time limits. But neither should you let yourself think that joy and laughter are over for you and your family. They aren't.

Each parent felt meaning, deep meaning, in their child's life, no matter how many months or years it lasted. All of them were grateful to have known their children, were grateful to have had them at all, even for a little while. Had any of them known of the pain and suffering they and their child would go through, and had they been able to prevent their child's birth, they all say they still would have chosen to have their child. The parents learned so much from their children (when they let them teach them) and saw so many lives touched and deepened by them. They saw their children, even very young children, deepen and grow from their experience. Often their wisdom was amazing. They gave their parents love and trusted them with their lives. Parents did the best they were capable of doing and feel grateful to their children for the time they spent with them.

For most parents their children are still alive in some way. They are alive in the hearts of those who loved them. They are alive in the lives they touched. They are alive in the totality of the cosmos, for as science tells us today, nothing is ever lost, just transformed. No particle of energy is extinguished, just converted. Those with a belief in an immortal soul feel that their child is still living and growing.

SUGGESTIONS

What would the parents tell another parent going through this?

Most parents emphasized the need to speak up and urge their peers not to be intimidated. Ask to read your child's medical record if you want to. (Most parents did want to, but didn't think it was allowed.) Question the treatments and procedures if you have doubts. Be honest with yourself and your child whenever you can.

Let yourself learn from your child. Forget once in a while that you are the parent, the authority, and let yourself go through the experience with your child as a fellow student, both learning together.

What would parents like to tell medical personnel and treatment centers?

Remember that you are treating children, fragile human beings, not machines. Show your humanity. Give the child, no matter how young, some explanation of what you are doing. Your efficiency won't suffer if you relate to the child with a smile or a word. Remember that the child, no matter how old, may be frightened by machinery and tests, and that fear does not aid healing. Relaxation and trust promote healing, and you can help by making the event less fearful. Include the parents whenever possible.

Make your treatment areas less grim. As one mother explained, "My two-year-old son was so frightened when he had echocardiograms, even though the examinations weren't painful. If only there had been puppets or mobiles or something for him to look at during the tests." Cheerful, soothing music could help too. These are not very expensive or time-consuming suggestions, but could be easily incorporated by medical personnel.

Above all, take the time to answer questions, even if you have answered them before. Many parents are under such stress that they may need further explanation. Neither you nor the parent are alone in wanting what is best for the child. You are working together for the child's well-being.

Appendix C

Agencies and Organizations That Help

American Cancer Society
777 Third Avenue
New York, New York 10017
(212) 371–2900

This national voluntary organization has many local branches throughout the country offering programs of cancer research and education. Services to patients include: information and referral for community health resources, equipment loans for home care, surgical dressings, and transportation. Other services may be available depending upon the local needs and resources. These services are without charge.

Assistance League
5627 Fernwood Avenue
Los Angeles, California 90028
(213) 469–5897

There are sixty-two local chapters in various states. Their purpose is to act as a friend to men, women, and children in order to aid physically, materially, and spiritually. Each center has a philanthropic purpose, but not all centers offer the same services. In some areas the service might include an emergency homemaker on a temporary basis (with costs on a sliding scale), a clothing bank, or other service. Some of these services could be useful to a family with a chronically ill child, but the parents would need to check with the local center to find out if an applicable service is offered.

Cancer Information Service
1-800-638-6694 (toll free)

This information service is supported by the National Cancer Institute.

Candlelighters Foundation
Suite 1011
2025 Eye Street, N.W.
Washington, D.C. 20006
(202) 659-5136

Candlelighters offer support for the whole family with a child who has cancer. They offer a twenty-four-hour crisis line, parent-to-parent contact, professional counseling, and self-help groups. Families are matched, and children are matched with other children. There are many other local group activities, so it is best to contact the national organization for the closest local group. Even if the family is not in the vicinity of a Candlelighters chapter, they can benefit from their publications: a newsletter, handbooks, and a teen newsletter.

Many groups have auxiliaries for teenage cancer patients and teenage siblings of children with cancer.

Candlelighters also has an information center that maintains a library and speakers bureau. All services and publications are free.

Center for Attitudinal Healing
19 Main St.
Tiburon, California 94920
(415) 435-5022

Bay Area groups support children, and families with children, who have a catastrophic illness. The Center participates in workshops locally and nationally to teach the Center's principles and to help those wishing to start other centers.

Visits to children and young adults in Bay Area hospitals offer support for the whole family. Meetings are arranged with the professionals involved in the child's health care, and there are also visits to schools. Center staff will also meet with the child's classmates and teachers.

The phone/pen pal program includes children, their siblings and parents, and adults with a catastrophic illness; it provides a network of support throughout the country. The Center matches children or adults with similar situations, depending upon their preference. You do not need to be in the Bay Area to participate.

All of the services at the Center are free of charge.

The Center also has an educational materials list; tapes, articles, and books prepared by the Center, or recommended by them, can be ordered. An outstanding example is *There is a Rainbow Behind Every Dark Cloud,* by the Children's Group, edited by Dr. Jerry Jampolsky and Pat Taylor (Celestial Arts, $5.95). Drawings and text by the children deal with their attitudes toward illness and death.

Crippled Children's Clinics

Crippled Children's Clinics exist in all but fifteen states. Though medical and financial qualifications vary from state to state, usually any congenital or posttraumatic disease or condition that could be crippling long range is covered, such as: cystic fibrosis, congenital heart defects, scoleosis, and some forms of cancer. The family receives financial help (on a sliding scale, also varying from region to region) for surgery, visits to physicians, hospital stays, X-rays, diagnostic tests, and three visits for psychiatric counseling (for children with a terminal illness). Even if a Crippled Children's Clinic is not available in the child's home city, as long as a clinic is in the state the parent may apply and may receive financial help for surgery or hospitalization. Also, if the services a qualified child needs are not available at the clinic, he may receive funds as an out-patient at another facility. Sometimes funds are available for needed equipment at home.

Though it is not possible to list every clinic, this list will cover the regions that do have a clinic and the address of the counselor for each region. Parents may check with the Health Department, or call Information and Referral (described in this Appendix), for local clinics.

REGION I (Connecticut, Maine, Massachusetts,
         New Hampshire, Rhode Island, Vermont)
    Counselor—M. Grace Hussey, M.D., Director
         Maternal and Child Health
         State Department of Public Health
         Division of Family Health Services
         39 Boylston Street
         Boston, Massachusetts 02116

REGION II (New Jersey, New York, Puerto Rico, Virgin Islands)
    Counselor—Fredrick Groff, M.D., Director
         Medical Rehabilitative Services
         State Department of Health
         Tower Building, Empire State Plaza
         Albany, New York 12220

REGION III (Delaware, District of Columbia, Maryland,
         Pennsylvania, Virginia, West Virginia)
    Counselor—Judson Force, M.D., Chief
         Division of Crippled Children's Services
         Department of Health and Mental Hygiene
         201 West Preston Street
         Baltimore, Maryland 21201

REGION IV (Alabama, Florida, Georgia, Kentucky, Mississippi,
         North Carolina, South Carolina, Tennessee)
    Counselor—Children's Medical Services
         Department of Health and Rehabilitative Services
         1323 Winewood Boulevard (Building 5-127)
         Tallahassee, Florida 32301

REGION V (Illinois, Indiana, Michigan, Minnesota, Ohio,
         Wisconsin)

Counselor—Horace K. Tenny III, M.D., Medical Director
Bureau of Crippled Children
State Department of Public Instruction
126 Langdon Street
Madison, Wisconsin 53702

REGION VI (Arkansas, Louisiana, New Mexico, Oklahoma, Texas)
Counselor—William J. Craig, M.D., Supervisor
Crippled Children's Unit
Department of Institutions, Social and
Rehabilitative Services
P.O. Box 25352
Oklahoma City, Oklahoma 73125

REGION VII (Iowa, Kansas, Missouri, Nebraska)
Counselor—Theodore Scurletis, M.D., Medical Director
Maternal and Child Health Services
State Department of Health
Lucas State Office Building
Des Moines, Iowa 50319

REGION VIII (Colorado, Montana, North Dakota, South Dakota, Utah, Wyoming)
Counselor—Robert S. McCurdy, M.D., Director
Family Health Services Division
State Department of Health
42190 East 11th Avenue
Denver, Colorado 80220

REGION IX (Arizona, California, Hawaii, Nevada, American Samoa, Guam, Trust Territory of the Pacific)
Counselor—Esmond S. Smith, M.D., Chief
Crippled Children's Services
State Department of Health
714–744 P Street
Sacramento, California 95814

REGION X (Alaska, Idaho, Oregon, Washington)
    Counselor—Victor D. Menashe, M.D., Director
                Crippled Children's Division
                University of Oregon Health Sciences Center
                P.O. Box 574
                Portland, Oregon 97207

Cystic Fibrosis Foundation
600 Executive Blvd.
Suite 309
Rockville, Maryland 20852

The Cystic Fibrosis Foundation has eighty-four local groups in this country devoted to research and public and professional education about cystic fibrosis, as well as care centers. Care centers provide outpatient medical aid (on a sliding scale) for damaging lung disorders such as cystic fibrosis, chronic bronchitis, and asthma in children and young adults. Gastro-intestinal diseases of children are also cared for. Local groups vary, and some other services may be provided, such as social activities for the patient and family, support groups for parents, and camping experiences for children.

Easter Seal Society
2023 West Ogden Ave.
Chicago, Illinois 60612

The Easter Seal Society is a service organization with branches throughout the country. The services provided locally vary tremendously, depending upon local needs. Some states have rehabilitation centers, while others offer transportation for the handicapped and equipment loan and purchase for those who need it. Some areas provide social activities for any child with a physical problem and camping experiences. Children with severe chronic diseases would be included and might benefit from recreational activities depending on the state of their illness. As the service varies from area to area, it is best for the parent to contact the local branch to find out what is available.

Information and Referral

There is no national number for Information and Referral, but most major cities offer this free telephone service, which also serves outlying areas. Information and Referral maintains up-to-date files of community services covering every area a family with a terminally ill child may need, such as: counseling, transportation, equipment loans, financial aid, medical service, etc. The local phone number is listed in the phone book under Information and Referral.

Leukemia Society of America, Inc.
211 East 43rd Street
New York, New York 10017
(212) 573-8484

Financial assistance, consultation, and referral to other means of local support are offered by chapters of the Leukemia Society of America to patients with leukemia and allied disorders. Coverage helps pay for drugs used in care, laboratory costs associated with blood transfusion, transportation, and part of the costs for X-ray therapy for early Hodgkin's disease and some of the costs for cranial radiation for children with acute lymphocytic leukemia. This assistance is available when these costs are not covered by other sources. For further information, however, it is best to contact the national office.

Loan Chests

The American Cancer Society funds Loan Chests of sickroom equipment in many areas. Sometimes other groups fund Loan Chests also, depending upon the local area. The service is usually free for patients cared for at home.

National Health Information Clearinghouse
1-800-336-4767 (toll free)

The National Health Information Clearinghouse answers any questions having to do with well-being and will try to find answers to your questions as well as the appropriate local organization or support group.

*Ronald McDonald House*_{TM}
National Coordinator
Golin/Harris Communications, Inc.
500 Michigan Ave.
Chicago, Illinois 60611
(312) 836-7129

There are thirty-two Ronald McDonald_{TM} houses open at this time, with thirty-four more on the way throughout this country, one in Canada and one in Sydney, Australia. Ronald McDonald_{TM} houses are temporary homes for parents and the families of children being treated for a serious illness. This is particularly necessary when parents have to commute some distance to the hospital and have to sleep in hospital lobbies or on cots and sofas to be near their child. Hotels are expensive for these families, and Ronald McDonald_{TM} houses ask only for a nominal donation, if the family can afford it. Children need their parents nearby, and Ronald McDonald_{TM} houses are located close to major treatment centers. Families meet informally and provide support for each other.

Appendix D

Hospice Programs for Children

National Hospice Organization
1311A Dolley Madison Boulevard
McLean, Virginia 22101
(703) 356-6770

It is best to contact the National Hospice Organization to find the closest local program as there are over five hundred new hospice programs in various stages of development. The hospice movement has experienced rapid growth in the past few years and though the tendency is for these programs to be based in a hospital, the emphasis is still on home care.

CHILDREN'S HOSPICE PROGRAMS

Children's Hospice Program
St. Mary's Hospital for Children
Bayside, New York

Boulder County Hospice, Inc.
2118 14th Street
Boulder, Colorado 80302
(303) 449-7740

The Connecticut Hospice Inc.
61 Burban Drive
Branford, Connecticut 06405
(203) 421-6231

Hospice of Northern Virginia
4715 N. 15th St.
Arlington, Virginia 22205
(703) 525-7070

Hospice of Louisville, Inc.
233 E. Gray St., Suite 800
Louisville, Kentucky 40202
(502) 584-4834

EDMARC—A Hospice for Children
   (severely disturbed and terminally
   ill)
P.O. Box 1684
Suffolk, Virginia 23434
(804) 539-2041

Appendix E

Home Care

If a home care program does not exist in your area, you and the treatment center or home health agency may work out arrangements for you to care for your child at home. The social worker or home care nurse can help coordinate efforts between the parents and health professionals and help arrange for necessary equipment such as hospital beds or wheelchairs or oxygen equipment.

There are several helpful texts for parents: *Home Care for Dying Children: A Manual for Parents* and *Home Care: A Manual for Implementation of Home Care for Children Dying of Cancer*, which may be ordered from:

> Research Center
> School of Nursing
> University of Minnesota
> 3313 Powell Hall
> 500 Essex St., S.E.
> Minneapolis, Minnesota 55455

Also: *Young People with Cancer: A Handbook for Parents*, U.S. Department of Health and Human Services, Public Health Service, National Institutes of Health, National Cancer Institute, Bethesda, Maryland 20205. This useful book can also be ordered through Candlelighters Foundation (see Appendix C).

Appendix F

Bereavement Support

Candlelighters Foundation
(See Appendix C) Self-help for parents who have or have had children with cancer.

Compassionate Friends
P.O. Box 1347
Oak Brook, Illinois 60521
This is a self-help organization offering support, friendship, and understanding for bereaved parents. The purposes are to aid parents in the positive resolution of the grief experienced upon the death of their child and to promote and foster the physical and emotional health of bereaved parents and siblings.

There are many local chapters (and related groups with other names). Check with the national address for the closest local group.

Hospice Programs
Many hospice programs offer bereavement support groups or bereavement counseling as part of their service to a patient's family. For information on local groups contact the National Hospice Organization (see Appendix D).

Notes

1. G.S. Konior, "The Fear of Dying: How Patients and Their Doctors Behave," *Seminars on Oncology* 2, no. 4 (1975): 311.
2. William J. Worden and William Proctor, *PDA: Personal Death Awareness* (Englewood Cliffs, N.J.: Prentice-Hall, 1976), p. 53.
3. Richard G. Dumont and Dennis C. Foss, *The American View of Death: Acceptance or Denial?* (Cambridge, Mass.: Schenkman, 1972), p. 20.
4. Joseph C. Rheingold, *The Mother, Anxiety, and Death: The Catastrophic Death Complex* (London: J. & A. Churchill, 1967), p. 49.
5. Herman Feifel and Lawrence T. Hermann, "Fear of Death in the Mentally Ill," *Psychological Reports* 33 (1973): 931.
6. Arnold Toynbee et al., eds., *Man's Concern with Death* (London: Hodder and Stoughton, 1968), p. 59.
7. Ronald Jay Cohen and Christian Parker, "Fear of Failure and Death," *Psychological Reports* 34 (1974): 54.
8. Robert Kastenbaum and Ruth Aisenberg, *The Psychology of Death* (New York: Springer, 1972).
9. Donald I. Templer, David Lester, and Carol F. Ruff, "Fear of Death and Femininity," *Psychological Reports* 35 (1974): 530.
10. J.R. Marshall, "The Geriatric Patient's Fear about Death," *Postgraduate Medicine* 57, no. 4 (1975): 144.
11. Herman Feifel and Allen B. Branscomb, "Who's Afraid of Death?" *Journal of Abnormal Psychology* 81 (1973): 286.
12. Marshall, p. 144.
13. Kastenbaum and Aisenberg, p. 84.
14. Feifel and Branscomb, "Who's Afraid of Death?" p. 282.
15. Dumont and Foss, p. 22.
16. Feifel and Branscomb, "Who's Afraid of Death?" p. 285.
17. Rheingold, p. 73.
18. Rheingold, p. 76.
19. Sylvia Anthony, *The Child's Discovery of Death: A Study in Child Psychology* (New York: Harcourt, Brace, 1940), p. 143.
20. Toynbee et al., p. 154.
21. Dumont and Foss, p. 28.
22. Thomas Hackett, "The Treatment of the Dying," *Journal of Pastoral Care* 2 (1964): 65.
23. Joseph Fletcher, *Morals in Medicine* (Princeton, N.J.: Princeton University Press, 1954), p. 50.
24. Colin M. Parkes, "The Patient's Right to Know the Truth," *Proceedings of the Royal Society of Medicine* 66 (1973): 537.

25. William Fitts and I.S. Raydin, "What Philadelphia Physicians Tell Patients with Cancer," *Journal of the American Medical Association* 153 (1953): 903.

26. W.D. Kelly and S.R. Friesen, "Do Cancer Patients Want to Be Told?" *Surgery* 27 (1950): 822–26.

27. Robert Samp and Anthony Curreri, "A Questionnaire Survey on Public Cancer Education Obtained from Patients and Their Families," *Cancer* 10 (1957): 382–84.

28. Elisabeth Kübler-Ross, *On Death and Dying* (New York: Macmillan Co., 1969), p. 29.

29. E.M. Litin, "Should the Cancer Patient Be Told?" *Postgraduate Medicine* 28 (1960): 473.

30. Joseph Fletcher, *Morals and Medicine* (Princeton: Princeton University Press, 1954), p. 48.

31. Litin, p. 473.

32. B.G. Glaser and A.L. Strauss, *Awareness of Dying* (Chicago: Aldine Press, 1965).

33. Raphael Ginzberg, "Should the Elderly Cancer Patient Be Told?" *Geriatrics* 4 (1949): 102.

34. J. Vernick and M. Karon, "Who's Afraid of Death on a Leukemia Ward?" *American Journal of Diseases of Children* 109 (1965): 396.

35. Geoffrey Gorer, *Death, Grief and Mourning* (Garden City, N.Y.: Doubleday, 1959), p. 10.

36. Robert Kastenbaum, "The Child's Understanding of Death: How Does It Develop?" in *Explaining Death to Children*, ed. Earl Grollman (Boston: Beacon Press, 1967), pp. 94–6.

37. Jeanne Benoliel, "The Terminally Ill Child," *Comprehensive Pediatric Nursing*, eds. Gladys Scipien, Martha Barnard, Marilyn Chard, Jeanne Howe, and Patricia Phillips (New York: McGraw-Hill, 1975), p. 427.

38. Ibid., p. 427.

39. Kastenbaum, pp. 101–106.

40. Bernard Rosenblatt, "Reactions of Children to the Death of Loved Ones—Some Notes Based on Psychoanalytic Theory," *The Loss of Loved Ones*, ed. D. Moriarty, (Springfield, Ill.: Charles C. Thomas, 1967), pp. 140–41.

41. Humberto Nagera, "Children's Reactions to the Death of Important Objects: A Developmental Approach," *Psychoanalytic Study of the Child* 25 (1970): 363.

42. Morris A. Wessel, "Death of an Adult and Its Impact upon the Child," *Clinical Pediatrics* 12 (1973): 31.

43. Ibid.

44. Martha Wolfenstein, "How Is Mourning Possible?" *Psychoanalytic Study of the Child* 21, (1966): 103–104.

45. Rebecca M. Hawener and Wallace Phillips, "The Grieving Child," *School Counselor* 22 (1975): 348.

46. Hendin, p. 153.

47. Richard A. Kalish, "The Effects of Death upon the Family," *Death and Dying*, ed. L. Pearson (Cleveland, 1969), p. 98.

48. John F. Schowalter, "How Do Children and Funerals Mix?" *Journal of Pediatrics* 89 (1976): 140–41.

49. Albert Krinsky, "Some Thoughts on Loss in Childhood," *The Loss of Loved Ones*, ed. D. Moriarty (Springfield, Ill.: Charles C. Thomas, 1967), p. 149.

50. Donald L. Weston and Robert C. Irwin, "Preschool Child's Response to Death of an Infant Sibling," *American Journal of Diseases of Children* 106 (1963): 565–66.

51. Audrey K. Gordon and Dennis Klass, *They Need to Know* (Englewood Cliffs, N.J.: Prentice-Hall, 1979), p. 6.

52. Ibid., p. 7

53. Joanne E. Bernstein, *Book to Help Children Cope with Separation and Loss* (New York: R.R. Bowker, 1977), p. 15.

54. National Institute of Mental Health, *Caring about Kids: Talking to Children about Death* (Washington, D.C.: Department of Health, Education and Welfare, 1979), p. 3.

55. Gordon and Klass, p. 27.

56. Ibid.
57. Ibid., p. 31.
58. Ibid., p. 32.
59. Earl A. Grollman, *Explaining Death to Children* (Boston: Beacon Press, 1967), p. 19.
60. Ibid.
61. Joanne E. Bernstein, *Book to Help Children Cope with Separation and Loss,* (New York: R.R. Bowker, 1977), pp. 12–13.
62. Ibid., pp. 14–15.
63. *A Cancer Source Book for Nurses,* American Cancer Society, 1975, pp. 1–3.
64. Joseph H. Burchenal, "Current Commentary I: Childhood Cancer," in *Clinical Management of Cancer in Children,* ed. Carl Pochedly (Acton, Mass.: Publishing Sciences Group, 1975), p. 1.
65. Stanford Friedman, Paul Chodoff, John Mason, and David Hamburg, "Behavioral Observations of Parents Anticipating the Death of a Child," in *Counselling Parents of the Ill and the Handicapped,* ed. Robert Noland (Springfield, Ill.: Charles Thomas, 1971), pp. 458–68.
66. Jo-Eileen Gyulay, *The Dying Child* (New York: McGraw-Hill, 1978), p. 8.
67. Barney Glaser and Anselm Strauss, *Awareness of Dying* (Chicago: Aldine, 1965), pp. 9–10.
68. Myra Bluebond-Langer, *The Private Worlds of Dying Children* (Princeton: Princeton University Press, 1978), p. 200.
69. Ibid., p. 197.
70. Ibid., p. 222.
71. Ibid., p. 222.
72. Peggy Chinn, *Child Health Maintenance* (St. Louis: C.V. Mosby, 1974), p. 434.
73. Friedman et al., p. 474.
74. Mary Anglim, "Reintegration of the Family after the Death of a Child," in *Home Care of the Dying Child—Professional and Family Perspectives,* ed. Ida Martinson (New York: Appleton-Century-Crofts, 1976), pp. 109–10.
75. Morris Green, "Care of the Child with a Long-Term, Life-Threatening Illness: Some Principles of Management," *Pediatrics* 39, no. 3 (1967): 444.
76. Gerald P. Koocher, "Talking with Children about Death," *American Journal of Ortho Psychiatry* 44, no. 3 (1974): 410.
77. Morris Powazek, "Emotional Reactions of Children to Isolation in a Cancer Hospital," *The Journal of Pediatrics* 92, no. 5 (1978): 836.
78. Ida M. Martinson, "Home Care for Children Dying of Cancer," *Pediatrics* 62, no. 1 (1978): 108.
79. Lupe-Rebeka Samaniego, "Exploring the Physically Ill Child's Self-Perceptions and the Mother's Perceptions of her Child's Needs," *Clinical Pediatrics* 16, no. 2 (1977): 157.
80. Ida M. Martinson, "When the Patient Is Dying: Home Care for the Child," *American Journal of Nursing* 77, no. 11 (1977): 1817.
81. Audrey E. Evans, "If a Child Must Die . . . ," *The New England Journal of Medicine* 278, no. 3 (1967): 139.
82. Martinson, "Home Care for Children Dying of Cancer," p. 110.
83. Ibid.
84. C.M. Binger, "Childhood Leukemia: Emotional Impact on Patient and Family," *The New England Journal of Medicine* 280, no. 8 (1968): 416.
85. Ida M. Martinson, "Introduction to the Home Care Project," in *Home Care of the Dying Child—Professional and Family Perspectives* (New York: Appleton-Century-Crofts, 1976), pp. 8–9.
86. Alice Graner, "The Effects of Pain on Child, Parent, and Health Professional," in *Home Care of the Dying Child—Professional and Family Perspectives,* ed. Ida Martinson (New York: Appleton-Century-Crofts; 1976), p. 68.

87. Martinson, "Introduction to the Home Care Project," p. 8.
88. Martinson, "Home Care for Children Dying of Cancer," p. 110; and "When the Patient Is Dying," p. 1817.
89. Reginald S. Lourie, "The Pediatrician and the Handling of Terminal Illness," *Pediatrics* 32, no. 4 (1963): 449.
90. Andre O. Lascari, "The Dying Child and the Family," *The Journal of Family Practice* 6, no. 6 (1978): 1281.
91. Ibid., p. 1284.
92. Martinson, "When the Patient Is Dying," p. 1817.
93. A.D. Hofmann, R.D. Becker, and H.P. Gabriel, *The Hospitalized Adolescent* (New York: The Free Press, 1976).
94. Ibid.
95. Moore, B.C. et al., "Psychological Problems in the Management of Adolescence with Malignancy," *Clinical Pediatrics* 8 (1969): 464–473.
96. Robert J. Lifton, *The Broken Connection* (New York: Simon and Schuster, 1979).
97. Elisabeth Kübler-Ross, *On Death and Dying* (New York: Macmillan, 1969).
98. Parkes Collin Murray, *Studies of Grief in Adult Life* (New York: International Universities Press, 1972), pp. 84–5.
99. Harriet S. Schiff, *The Bereaved Parent* (New York: Crown, 1977).
100. Rollo May, *The Meaning of Anxiety*, quoted in "The Guilt of Parents of Children with Severe Physical Disease," R. Gardner, *American Journal of Psychiatry* 126 (1969): 5.
101. Glenn Vernon, *A Time to Die* (Washington: University Press of America, 1977).
102. C.E. Orbach, "The Multiple Meanings of the Loss of a Child," *American Journal of Psychotherapy* 13 (1959): 906.
103. E.N. Jackson, *The Christian Funeral* (New York: Channel Press, 1966).
104. Rebecca M. Hawener, "The Grieving Child," *The School Counselor* (May 1975): 347–51.
105. Lily Pincus, *Death and the Family* (New York: Pantheon Books, 1974), p. 158.
106. Sula Wolff, *Children Under Stress* (New York: Penguin Press, 1969), p. 53.
107. Edgar N. Jackson, *Telling a Child About Death* (New York: Hawthorn Books, 1965), p. 16.
108. Richard C. Nelson, "Helping Children to Cope with Death," *Elementary School Guidance and Counseling* (March 1975): 226.
109. Audrey K. Gordon, *They Need to Know—How to Teach Children About Death and Dying* (Englewood Cliffs, N.J.: Prentice-Hall, Inc., 1979), p. 100.
110. Gretchen Mills, *Discussing Death—A Guide to Death Education* (Palm Springs, Ca.: ETC Publications, 1976), p. 33.
111. David Barton, M.D., *A Clinical Guide for Caregivers* (n.p., n.d.), p. 67.
112. Edwin S. Schneidman, "You and Death," *Psychology Today* (June 1971): 44.
113. Pincus, p. 129.
114. Colarusso, Calvin, "Johnny Did Your Mother Die?" *Teacher* (February 1975): 57.
115. *Death Education* (Washington, D.C.: Hemisphere Publishing Corp., 1978), p. 295.
116. Mills, p. 46.
117. Morris Green, "Care of the Child with a Long-Term, Life-Threatening Illness: Some Principles of Management," *Pediatrics* 39, no. 3 (1967).
118. Stanford B. Friedman, "Behavioral Observations of Parents Anticipating the Death of the Child," *Pediatrics* 32, no. 3 (1963).

Selected Bibliography

Anthony, Sylvia. *The Child's Discovery of Death: A Study in Child Psychology*. New York: Harcourt, Brace, and Company, 1940.

Benton, Richard. *Death and Dying*. New York: Van Nostrand Reinhold, 1978.

Berstein, Joanne E. *Book to Help Children Cope with Separation and Loss*. New York: R. R. Bowker Company, 1977.

Bradley, Buff. *Endings—A Book About Death*. Reading, Massachusetts: Addison-Wesley Publishing Co., 1979.

Burton, L., ed. *Care of the Child Facing Death*. London: Routledge and Kegan Paul, 1974.

Colarusso, Calvin. "Johnny Did Your Mother Die?" *Teacher*, February 1975, p. 57.

Cook, Sarah Sheets. *Children and Dying*. New York: Health Sciences Publishing Corp., 1974.

Daniel, W. A., Jr. *Adolescents in Health and Disease*. St. Louis: C. V. Mosby, 1977.

Dempsey, P., *The Way We Die*. New York: Macmillan, 1975.

Dumont, Richard G. and Dennis C. Foss. *The American View of Death: Acceptance or Denial?* Cambridge, Mass.: Schenkman, 1972.

Easson, W. M. *The Dying Child*. Springfield, Ill.: Charles C. Thomas, 1970.

Evans, Audrey E. "If a Child Must Die . . . " *The New England Journal of Medicine* 278, no. 3 (1967): 138–42.

Feifel, Herman and Allan B. Branscomb. "Who's Afraid of Death?" *Journal of Abnormal Psychology* 81 (1973): 282–88.

Feifel, Herman. *The Meaning of Death*. New York: McGraw-Hill Co., 1959.

Frelund, Delphia J. "Children and Death from the School Setting Viewpoint." *The Journal of School Health* 47 (1977): 533–37.

Furman, Robert A. "A Child's Capacity for Mourning." In *The Child in His Family: The Impact of Death and Disease*, edited by E. J. Anthony and C. Koupernik. New York: John Wiley and Sons, 1973, 225–230.

Fletcher, Joseph. *Morals and Medicine*. Princeton: Princeton University Press, 1954.

Glaser, B. G. and Strauss, A. L. *Awareness of Dying*. Chicago: Aldine Press, 1965.

Goodman, Soll. "The Special Needs of Bereaved Children." In *But Not to Lose*, edited by A. Kutscher. New York: Frederick Fell, 1969, pp. 158–62.

Gordon, Audrey K. and Klass Dennis. *They Need to Know*. Englewood Cliffs, N. J.: Prentice-Hall, 1979.

Gorer, Geoffrey. *Death, Grief and Mourning*. Garden City, N. Y.: Doubleday, 1965.

Grollman, Earl A., *Explaining Death to Children*. Boston: Beacon Press, 1967.

Grant, Wilson W. "What Parents of a Chronically Ill or Dysfunctioning Child Always Wanted to Know but May Be Afraid to Ask." *Clinical Pediatrics* 17, no. 12 (1978): 915–17.

Hawener, Rebecca M. and Wallace Phillips. "The Grieving Child." *The School Counselor*, May 1975, pp. 347–51.

Hendin, David. *Death as a Fact of Life*. New York: W. W. Norton, 1973.

Hodge, J. R. "How to Help Your Patients Approach the Inevitable." *Medical Times* 102 (1974): 123–33.

Hofmann, A. D., R. D. Becker, and H. P. Gabriel. *The Hospitalized Adolescent*. New York: The Free Press, 1976.

Hollingsworth, Charles E. *The Family in Mourning—A Guide for Health Professionals*. New York: Grune and Stratton, 1977.

Inhelder, B. and J. Piaget. *The Growth of Logical Thinking from Childhood to Adolescence*. New York: Basic Books, Inc., 1958.

Jackson, Edgar N. *Telling a Child about Death*. New York: Hawthorn Books, 1965.

Jackson, E. N. *The Christian Funeral*. New York: Channel Press, 1966.

Kastenbaum, Robert and Ruth Aisenberg. *The Psychology of Death*. New York: Springer, 1972.

Kastenbaum, Robert J. *Death, Society, and Human Experience*. St. Louis: C. V. Mosby, 1977.

Klein, Melanie. In *The Way We Die*, by P. Dempsey. New York: Macmillan, 1975.

Krinsky, Albert, "Some Thoughts on Loss in Childhood." In *The Loss of Loved Ones*, edited by D. Moriarty. Springfield, Ill.: Charles C. Thomas, 1967, pp. 146–50.

Kübler-Ross, Elisabeth. *On Death and Dying*. New York: Macmillan, 1969.

Kübler-Ross, Elisabeth. "The Child Will Always Be There: Real Love Doesn't Die." *Psychology Today* 10 (1978): 48.

Lepp, Ignace. *Death and Its Mysteries*. New York: Macmillan, 1968.

Lifton, R. J. *The Broken Connection*. New York: Simon and Schuster, 1979.

Lowenburg, J. S. "The Coping Behaviors of Fatally Ill Adolescents and Their Parents." *Nursing Forum* 9: 269–87.

Lund, Charles C. "The Doctor, the Patient and the Truth." *Annals of Internal Medicine* (June 1946).

Maxwell, M. B. "A Terminally Ill Adolescent and Her Family." *American Journal of Nursing* 72 (1972): 925–27.

Mayerson, Evelyn Wilde. *Putting the Ill at Ease*. New York: Harper and Row, 1976.

Martinson, Ida M. "Home Care for Children Dying of Cancer." *Pediatrics* 62, no. 1 (1978): 106–13.

Martinson, Ida M. "When the Patient Is Dying: Home Care for the Child." *American Journal of Nursing* 77, no. 11 (1977): 1815–17.

Mills, Gretchen. *Discussing Death—A Guide to Death Education*. Palm Springs, Ca.: ETC Publications, 1976.

Morgenthau, J. E., ed. *Adolescent Health Care: A Multidisciplinary Approach*. Stanford, Conn: Thrush Press, 1976.

National Institute of Mental Health. *Caring About Kids: Talking to Children About Death*. Washington, D. C.: Department of Health, Education and Welfare, 1979.

Nottingham, E. K. *Religion: A Sociological View*. New York: Random House, 1971.

Nelson, Richard C. and William D. Peterson, "Challenging the Last Great Taboo: Death." *School Counselor* 22 (1975): 353–358.

Parkes, Colin M. *Bereavement: Studies of Grief in Adult Life*. New York: International Universities Press, 1972.

Pincus, Lily. *Death and the Family*. New York: Pantheon Books, 1974.

Reich, R. and H. B. Feinberg. "The Fatally Ill Adolescent." *Adolescent Psychiatry* 3 (1974): 75–83.

Rheingold, Joseph C. *The Mother, Anxiety, and Death: The Catastrophic Death Complex*. London: J. & A. Churchill, 1967.

Robinson, J. A., and Colin M. Parkes. "The Patient's Right to Know the Truth." *Proceedings of the Royal Society of Medicine* 66 (1973): 536–37.

Robinson, Mary Evans. "When a Child Dies." In *But Not to Lose,* edited by A. Kutscher. New York: Frederick Fell, 1969, pp. 107–12.

Rosenblatt, Bernard. "Reactions of Children to the Death of Loved Ones—Some Notes Based on Psychoanalytic Theory." In *The Loss of Loved Ones,* edited by D. Moriarty. Springfield, Ill.: Charles C. Thomas, 1967, pp. 135–45.

Schiff, Harriet S. *The Bereaved Parent.* New York: Crown, 1977.

Tanner, Ira J. *The Gift of Grief.* New York: Hawthorn Books, 1976.

Toynbee, Arnold, et al., eds. *Man's Concern with Death.* London: Hodder and Stoughton, 1968.

Veatch, Robert. *Death, Dying and the Biological Revolution.* New Haven: Yale University Press, 1976.

Vernon, Glenn. *A Time to Die.* Washington, D.C.: The University Press of America, 1977.

Wolff, Sula. *Children Under Stress.* London: Allen Lane/Penguin Press, 1969.

Wolman, Benjamin. *Psychoanalysis and Catholicism.* New York: Gardner Press, 1976.

Worden, William J. and William Proctor. *PDA: Personal Death Awareness.* Englewood Cliffs, N.J.: Prentice-Hall, 1976.

Zeligs, Rose. *Children's Experience with Death.* Springfield, Ill.: Charles C. Thomas, 1974.